My Journey Through the Twentieth Century

by

Governor Frank B. Morrison

D1567377

My Journey Through the Twentieth Century

—————————— *by* ——————————

Governor Frank B. Morrison

Media Productions and Marketing, Inc.

Lincoln, Nebraska

Media Productions and Marketing, Inc.
2622 Nottingham Court
Lincoln, NE 68512

ISBN 1-893453-09-X

5 4 3 2 1

Photos courtesy of Frank B. Morrison

Cover and book design by Reynold Peterson
Advance production by Eagle Printing, Lincoln, NE
Proof and Editing by Morgan Wright

DEDICATION

This book is dedicated to and in acknowledgement of the debt I owe
my mother, my aunt, my wife, my family, my teachers and others who have
inspired and helped me on my trip through the twentieth century...

AND

To the indomitable human spirit which contains within its soul
the capacity to elevate the quality of human life on this planet to heights
heretofore unknown and ever more worthy of immortality...

AND

To that seed that resides within the human heart to pursue perfection.

Contents

Preface

Nebraska's twentieth century history is inseparably entwined with a truly remarkable individual: The Honorable Frank B. Morrison, three term Governor of the State of Nebraska.

As a teacher, political leader, counselor and confidant of thousands, husband, father, grandfather and Nebraskan par excellence, he is leaving his mark on all of us whether or not we fully understand that.

To me he is a second father and a source of pride and inspiration. He established a political act that is hard to follow and impossible to surpass.

As a decent human being he has no peer. Even in the hotbed and aftermath of political wars, I never knew him to hold a grudge. He is a true believer in "do unto others". After he was first elected Governor, we were discussing whether or not to retain a department head who served in the previous administration and who said many unkind and untruthful things about Morrison in the primary contest. During the deliberations Morrison seemed unconcerned and when we reminded him about the things he said, his response was, "but what has he said about us lately?"

Frank Morrison is one of a cadre of exceptional leaders to emerge from the rural community of McCook, Nebraska. Among others were George Norris, Ralph Brooks, Gene Budig, Harry Strunk and most recently, Ben Nelson.

Governor Morrison was a confidant of Presidents Kennedy and Johnson. He was called to the White House immediately after the assassination of President Kennedy.

His words of wisdom and tales of humor and self-deprecation and accomplishments are not only entertaining but also a factual portrayal of a gifted and dedicated Nebraskan.

A sincere regret I have is that he never served his State and Nation in the United States Senate. Maybe he's saving that for the twenty-first century.

J. James Exon, Lincoln, Nebraska, March, 2001

There is a place where glaciers sculpt granite and

ivory beargrass clouds spring from splashing of
paintbrush and lilies.

Where big horn sheep scale timeless citadels,

ladled with lakes of God's own nectar,

where rainbows jump three feet high and crashing
cascades forbid the untempered

where rich land reaches up to embrace its people, and

people reach out reverently to touch the land.

Where strangers are friends and friends are brothers.

Where individuals are not lost in an anxious sea of
humanity

where life itself is joyous adventure.

To know that land and live its promise is to taste
life's finest wine.

— John Morrison

Habitat for Humanity

As if for the first time, I awakened from a deep sleep to a condition I call consciousness - a condition that enabled me to see, hear, remember, reason, and wonder why. It was early morning, July 2, 1997, and we were vacationing in Whitefish, Montana. Whitefish was surrounded by rugged mountains laced with beautiful streams and lakes. Modern high speed transportation had made this terrain accessible to the inhabitants of the high plains and provided an inspiring diversity for man to enjoy.

The sun was just coming up in Glacier National Park. The corn, wheat, and grasslands of the Great Plains were sprouting. As I witnessed this sight, I knew that the fish, deer, elk, and mountain lions that inhabited these mountains, and the prairie dogs, beaver, bison, and ground squirrels that inhabited the Great Plains had not changed their habits in thousands of years. I then thought of this anxious sea of humanity. How have we changed? What is our future?

Later that day, our son, Frank Brenner Morrison Jr., nicknamed Biff after a legendary Nebraska football coach,[1] drove us the nine miles from Whitefish to Glacier International Airport in Montana's Northern Rockies. Biff, a fourth generation product of America's Great Plains, and his wife, Sharon, loved the mountains. They had decided this was where they wanted to live and raise their two children. Their son, John, was only in the third grade when the family moved to Montana. The environment made a lasting impression on him. Although, as an adult, he became a prominent Montana lawyer, the lyricist in him penned the tribute to the environment that opens this story.

As my wife Maxine, my son, and I waited at the airport for that great jet-powered airplane to take us through the summer sky to Salt Lake City and thence to Omaha, almost half a continent away, my mind went back to my own childhood. There, before my mind's eye, appeared the world of my first consciousness:

my mother taking a horse from the barn, placing her between the shafts of a buggy and taking off for town. The ten mile trip would take her about the same time it would take us now to fly across the continent. Communications, which used to take months to deliver, could now take place in seconds. Diseases, which meant death in those days, are now curable. It was a different world.

To try and comprehend my awareness of this world around me was to dominate my consciousness from age five until my death. Therefore, I shall attempt, in the following pages, to relate some of my experiences in this realm of consciousness.

*   *   *

Perhaps my readers should first learn something about the forebears who brought me to this realm of consciousness.

The Morrison family who settled in the colony of New York was of Scottish-rish stock. My grandfather, Milton John Morrison, son of Caldwell Morrison and Elizabeth Osborne Cottrell, was born in St. Louis, Missouri. When Milton was three years of age, the family moved to Margan County, Illinois which, by the late 1830s, became part of Scott County, Illinois. Here, Caldwell Morrison and his family became prominent farmers and extensive landowners. Caldwell died in 1851; his wife died two years later.

In 1853, Milton married Mary Carroll Davis. Two sons, Caldwell and Reverdy, were born to them. In 1859, news of the gold strike in Colorado lured Milton to acquire a yoke of oxen, one cow, and a covered wagon for a trip to Gold Country. The cow did double duty by helping to pull the wagon and furnishing milk for the trip. Butter was churned from the jiggle of the wagon as it bumped over the rough roads.

After a short stay in what is now Denver, Milton and his family moved up Coal Creek near Boulder to Gold Hill where they camped near a stream named Gold Run. This was fortuitous because their wagon was saved from a destructive fire with water from the creek.

That fall, the family moved to Central City where Milton supported his family by hauling hay and supplies to the mining camps. During the winter of 1860, the family operated a large log rooming house at the foot of Guy Hill on the Golden Gate Road.

In 1864, Milton took up a preemption claim four miles west of Arvada that was located on the high ground on the left side of the creek. This land had been passed over repeatedly until the farmers learned they could bring water to it. In 1865, the year of my father's birth, Milton and his neighbors built an irrigation ditch known as the Ralston, Golden, and Clear Creek Ditch.

The next year Milton first took a homestead on the north side of Ralston Creek and later acquired one east of Longmont on the St. Vrain River. After moving to Colorado, Milton and his wife increased their family by three more boys: Frank, my father; Abraham Lincoln; and Edward. It was in this environment of farming, irrigating, and building ditches around Golden, Colorado that my father was reared.

When the state established a school of mines at Golden, my father took engineering courses and became obsessed with irrigation. Meanwhile, my father married, started a family, and built two different homes near Golden. Sadly, his wife suffered a long illness, died, and left my father a widower with two small daughters.

Then, Viva Montez Brenner entered his life. I shall tell you more about my mother later. My father died three and a half years after their marriage. He had traveled from Golden to Scottsbluff, Nebraska to inspect potential for irrigation. Shortly before his death, he wrote my mother from Mitchell, Nebraska telling her how impressed he was with Scottsbluff. It reminded him a great deal of Boulder.

After his death, my mother took a homestead under a new ditch on the high land north of Brush, Colorado because the South Platte River Valley was now teeming with irrigation. Here on eastern Colorado's old frontier I was first introduced to consciousness. Here I became conscious of nature's mysteries. I remember the plant and animal life, the sound of the wind, the howl of the coyotes at night, the chirp of prairie dogs by day, and the mighty sea of rolling tumbleweeds in the fall. The fact that water, sunshine, soil, and plant seed could produce a beautiful plant was wondrous.

Here, too, my value system was born - a value system of hard work, dedication, and a vision of working with nature to improve the human condition. My son, Biff, characterized this ideal on my 70th birthday with these words:

> *Colorado's arid and untamed land*
> *where wind bent grass scratched the sky*
> *and nature's wrath forged a union of earth and man*
> *a father's dream of barren soil*
> *married to the mountain water source*
> *forever changing the prairie's face*
> *rewarding years of arduous toil*
> *a mother undaunted by deprivation*
> *armed with courage and iron will*
> *left to her ancestral line*
> *a legacy of self determination.*

1 The coach was Lawrence "Biff" McCeney Jones. During his professional career (1926-1941) he coached at Army, Louisiana State, Oklahoma and Nebraska. As head coach at the University of Nebraska from 1937-1941, he compiled a record of 28 wins, 14 losses, and 4 ties. His teams also won two conference titles. "Biff" Jones was inducted into the College Football Hall of Fame in 1954.

Viva Brenner Morrison

A Mother Who Risked Her Life To Give Me Birth

Who was this woman of iron will who left to her progeny a legacy of self-determination?[2]

Viva Montez Brenner was born on April 20, 1875 in Bourbon County, Kansas. Her mother, Charlotte Smith, was of Scottish-Irish descent. Her father was Jacob Brenner, a farmer whose passion was politics. As a Republican, he served many years as a county commissioner. Later, while serving in the Kansas Legislature, he helped write the first women's suffrage plank for his party's platform.

When Jacob was twelve years old, the Adam Brenner family[3] moved to Shannon, Illinois and became farmers in that area. Here my grandfather, Jacob, lived until he enlisted in the Civil War from nearby Freeport. He was shot in the right hand at the battle of Champion Hill during the siege of Vicksburg. Only one finger and a thumb were left on his right hand. After the war, he homesteaded in Bourbon County, Kansas. Here he met and married a local school teacher from Ohio, Charlotte Smith.[4] Jacob and Charlotte Brenner had four children: Viva, Tice, George, and Flora. Although Jacob and Charlotte never attended college, they were eager for their children to have a good education.

Sometime after the Civil War, the State of Kansas converted Bluemont College in Manhattan, Kansas into a land grant agricultural college.[5] At the turn of the century the Brenners rented a house in Manhattan for their now college-age children. The boys were to study scientific agriculture and the girls were to study domestic science. The girls were also expected to do the cooking and house-

keeping. The boys got married and failed to take advantage of the college opportunities. The girls completed college and obtained bachelor's degrees in domestic
science. In the meantime, the Brenners sold their Bourbon County farm and purchased a small farm on Wildcat Creek some two miles west of Manhattan.

In 1903, Viva was a beautiful young woman of twenty-eight with long brown
curly hair which, when left to hang loose, fell to her waist. She had finished three
years of college when she journeyed to Golden, Colorado to spend the summer
with an aunt and uncle. These relatives had a neighbor named Frank Morrison
whose wife had recently died and left him with two young girls.

As a neighborly act, Viva began helping out with the two little girls, Hazel and
Florence. Viva quickly became indispensable to the young widower ten years her
senior. He proposed marriage before the summer ended. Viva consented on one
condition, that she first return to Manhattan and finish her last year of college.

The following year, on June 28, 1904, they were married at the Brenner farm
outside Manhattan. Then the new couple returned to Frank's home at Golden,
Colorado. Overnight, the young bride found herself responsible for a husband
and two young daughters.

On May 20, 1905, a son, Frank Brenner Morrison, was born. The next year
a daughter, Eva Hope, was born on May 31, 1906. Little did this happy family
know that the following year, the father would contract a fatal case of pneumonia
and die, leaving Viva with two babies and two teenage daughters.

Following this tragedy, the young widow decided to strike out on her own.
Her husband had been interested in the eastern Colorado frontier. A new irrigation canal had been built on the high land north of the South Platte River near
Snyder, Colorado. Viva took a homestead in the area. While her house on the
homestead was being built, she rented a house in Brush, a town about ten miles
southeast. Though Snyder was five miles closer than Brush to the homestead,
Snyder did not have a high school and my older sisters were then of high school
age. Hazel was married on the homestead shortly after graduation. Later, Florence
became engaged to a neighbor boy.

By 1911, Viva learned that her aging parents were in poor health and needed
her. She returned to their farmhouse west of Manhattan where she had been married seven years before. It was on this farm that the true physical and emotional
strength of this young woman was tested. The farm was bisected by Wildcat Creek
and the main line of the Rock Island Railroad. This situation created a kid's paradise but mother's headache.

Jacob Brenner, Viva's father, was too old to operate the farm, and his wife was
suffering from pernicious anemia. The farmhouse contained no central heating or
plumbing. Water was carried to the house in a bucket filled from a shallow hand-
dug well between the house and the barn. Kerosene lamps provided light. An out-

Jacob Brenner, father of my mother and Aunt with old cronies. (third from left)
His crippled hand was my inspiration for public service.

Aunt Flora Edna Brenner Snyder   *Mother Viva Brenner Morrison*
The two women who charted the early course of my life.

door privy was fifty feet from the house. The farm was stocked with three horses, six milk cows, hogs, chickens, and a number of dogs and cats. Young Frank soon learned to do the chores and take care of the animals.

Viva's mother, Charlotte, died in 1915. Jacob became an invalid from prostate surgery. In 1916, the farm was traded for a house in Manhattan. Here Viva nursed her invalid father, operated the house, held down a full-time job at the college, and served as parent to two young children. In 1919, Jacob died.

Viva's chief goal after that was to see that her children acquired a college education. In the middle of the forties, Viva retired from her position as buyer and storekeeper for the College of Domestic Science at Kansas State. At that time, there was no pension, social security, or Medicare, but she lived an active and productive life. In 1949, Viva moved to McCook, Nebraska where she helped her divorced daughter, Hope, with housekeeping and parenting chores. Hope held a full-time job as an LPN at St. Catherine's Hospital in McCook. Viva died in Lincoln on her wedding anniversary in 1964 as a result of complications from cancer surgery.

Viva Brenner Morrison, who had been a widow for fifty-seven years, had devoted all of that time to serving others. The Nebraska Highway Patrol escorted her body to the Colorado line where they were met by the Colorado Highway Patrol under orders from the Governor of Colorado. She was buried next to her husband, Frank, in the family cemetery at Longmont, Colorado.

What was there about my mother, Viva Montez Brenner Morrison, that inspired her grandson Biff Morrison to write a poem to her memory referring to her as a mother of "courage and iron will who left to her ancestral line a legacy of self-determination?" What was there about this woman that caused the Nebraska Highway Patrol to give her the honor of escorting her body to the Colorado border? What was there about this woman that caused the Governor of Colorado to order his Highway Patrol to meet her body at the Nebraska border and escort it to Longmont for burial beside her husband? It was probably a combination of things.

First, there was the fact that her father-in-law was a Colorado pioneer. My father was born there before the City of Denver existed. In an age when few women insisted on a college degree for themselves, my mother did. Both of her children were born in Colorado. She became a mother to her husband's two daughters by his deceased first wife. She always placed duty above self.

On May 20, 1905, in Golden, Colorado, she was about to give birth to her first child, a thirteen-and-a-half pound boy. The birth would endanger her life, but she refused to consider partial birth abortion. The original doctor gave up and called in another. Thus, Frank Brenner Morrison was born and Viva Brenner

Frank Brenner Morrison

Morrison survived the ordeal.

As a widow, she braved the wild, undeveloped eastern Colorado frontier. When her aging parents became old and ill, she went to them, nursed them, and sustained them while caring for her own children. She had a moral code by which she lived and raised her children. She experienced poverty and deprivation but remained steadfast in her goal to see that her children received love, care, and a good education. She never received a pension, Medicare, or social security. She supported herself to the very end. She saw her only son become governor of a state bordering Colorado, which no doubt inspired the respect of the Colorado governor. She was the embodiment of humility, never seeking recognition or glory for herself. In an age when far too many people abandon responsibility for dependency, blame others for their failures, do what gives them a pleasant sensation, and fail to become role models for their children, the life of Viva Brenner Morrison became a compass for her family, her community, and those in authority. My son refers to her legacy as "self-determination." Though she has passed from the realm of consciousness, for our family, me, and countless others, the impact of her life will never die.

2 Ethel Fountain, wife of General Fountain, Adjutant General of the Iowa National Guard and District Judge in Des Moines, Iowa, was a first cousin of Viva Morrison. She compiled a genealogy of mother's ancestry on the Brenner side going back to 1737. This was the ancestry that produced two of the women who would shape my life forever, Viva Montez Morrison and her sister, Flora Edna Brenner Snyder.

3 Gerhardt Brenner came to Philadelphia in 1737. He migrated from the German part of Switzerland, came down the Rhine River, and sailed to Philadelphia from Rotterdam. He settled in the Pennsylvania Dutch country of Pennsylvania. His grandson, Adam Brenner, was born in Lancaster County, Pennsylvania, April 8, 1804. Adam married Suzanne Yorty; among their children was my grandfather, Jacob Brenner, who was born in 1839.

4 My grandmother was born Charlotte Angeline Smith in Athens, Ohio on December 29, 1849. She was the daughter of Samuel Smith and Fannie Davis. Charlotte was born in Ohio in 1818, we have no records beyond that.

5 This agricultural college was first known as Kansas State Agricultural College. The name was later changed to Kansas State University. It was endowed by Congress in 1862 under the Morrill Act. This law gave to the states thirty thousand acres of land for each senator and congressman, which land could be sold and the proceeds used to finance education in agriculture, mechanical arts (engineering), domestic science, and military training. This legislation, for the first time in history, provided a three-pronged approach to education: instruction, research, and demonstration. It laid the foundation for America's pre-eminence in agriculture, engineering, and the domestic sciences such as food, clothing, and housing. No more important act was ever passed by Congress.

A Kid on Wildcat Creek

The year 1912 was a landmark year in our country's history and an interesting year in the life of Frank Brenner Morrison. The unsinkable ship, Titanic, sank. Arizona was admitted to the Union. Teddy Roosevelt split the Republican Party wide open with his Bull Moose progressive movement,[6] and Woodrow Wilson, a Democrat, was elected President.

While these events registered in my consciousness, they were not as significant to me as my first full year on Wildcat Creek. My consciousness of the world around me expanded greatly. I became acquainted with domestic animals, discovered where milk came from, and learned to take it from the cows. I learned to saddle and ride a horse, herd the cows, and take them to and from the pasture. The cows were milked in the barn which, in the summer heat, produced an abundance of flies. Many of the flies were so irritating to the cows, they would try to swat them with their tails. Occasionally, the cow's urine-soaked tail would hit me in the face. It was inevitable that some of the dirt, manure, and urine from the cow would fall into the milk bucket. When the three-gallon pail was nearly full, it was carried to the porch. There, the dirt was strained out with a dish towel and the milk was poured into a hand-powered cream separator. I learned to operate the separator, save the cream and some of the skim milk for table use, and take the balance to the pigpen where this precious commodity was ravenously consumed by the pigs. In those days, skim milk had no commercial value except for hog feed. Pasteurization and homogenization were unknown to us. The contaminated raw milk was used with no ill effects.

While this raw milk might leave something to be desired in the area of sanitation, life on the Brenner farm was a kid's paradise. The main line of the Rock Island Railroad was hardly a hundred yards from the house, carrying passengers from the far reaches of America. On the other side of that railroad was the playground of my childhood, Wildcat Creek. This stream was home to many species of fish, frogs, and muskrats. Here I learned to fish, play in the cool fresh water, and listen to the birds sing. These things were to become an indelible part of my life. On a hot summer night, I would sit in the yard intoxicated with the glow of fireflies that lent the magic of twinkling light to the dark of the night. I gazed into the endless starlit skies uncontaminated with automobile exhaust. I accepted as commonplace the wonder of it all but, as I learned from my grandmother's Bible, human beings were stewards and trustees of it all, to protect and preserve.

The farm animals were my friends. I learned to ride the horses and hitch them to a buggy or wagon. I learned to hitch them to a mower and take them to an alfalfa field just west of the house. Here the sickle bar, powered by this horse-drawn machine, would cut the crop. When it was dry, a horse-drawn rake would compile it into rows called windrows. Days later, we would harness the horses to a wagon called a hayrack to collect the dry alfalfa and take it to the barn.

Our barn was a two-story affair. The top story was the hayloft. There was a large door which opened from the hayloft to the outside in order to receive the hay. At the top of the loft was a pulley attached to a rail. This pulley was operated with a rope, the other end of which was attached to a gigantic fork whose jaws could be opened or closed by another smaller rope. The larger rope, after going through the pulley, passed through the open door to the ground where another pulley conducted it to a piece of wood called a single tree. This was buckled to the harness of the horse and was designed to pull the fork from the ground to the hay-mow. The open jaws of the hay fork would descend to the loaded hayrack below, grab a fork full of hay, then close its jaws while the horse-drawn rope would lift the hay into the barn. There, a man at the other end of the smaller rope would pull, open the fork's jaws, and deposit the hay in the loft where it was stored. Later, the hay would be pitched through a hole in the loft to the animals below.

The year 1915 was the wettest on record. I distinctly remember two different evenings as I was carrying the skimmed milk,[7] a bank of clouds was lying low in the northwest. As I lay in my bed the following night, I was awakened by constant thunder. The sky outside my bedroom window was aglow with sheet lightening. When morning came, I heard the roar of rampaging waters. What excitement! Wildcat Creek had escaped its banks and the yellow water carrying dead trees and other debris had invaded our cornfield south of the house. The destructive power of nature was adding excitement to rural life. Thus, I learned that nature can be destructive as well as creative.

I loved and enjoyed the company of the farm animals, riding the horses, exploring the woods on the south end of the farm, and listening to the sounds and songs of birds. Still, something was missing. I longed for the company of other children. My sister, Hope, did not entirely fill this need. By nature, I was a people person. My greatest pleasure during those days on Wildcat Creek was when I could play with my cousins. Raymond Brenner, who lived with his parents in Manhattan, was four years my junior. His sister, Verniece, was born years later.

Raymond was the son of George and Eltie Brenner. George was my mother's eccentric brother. He owned a blind horse which he hitched to a wagon for the purpose of bringing the family to the farm for a visit. This horse was also used to power a homemade cider mill in his backyard. George converted his wife's kitchen into a place to make jelly and jam and grind horseradish which he would sell on the streets of Manhattan.

Raymond was a pleasant, happy playmate. He loved people and they loved him. He was almost a clone of his short, pleasant, lovely, pigeon-toed mother. His visits to the farm were all too infrequent for my taste. After working his way through high school, he left for California where he still lives. He used his personal charm to become a civic leader and labor union official. Raymond never knew a stranger. He learned business early in life. When about four years of age, he entered a variety store to buy some candy and asked the owner to charge it. When the owner refused, Raymond notified him that hereafter, he would take his business elsewhere.

My mother's brother, Tice, rented the farm immediately to the east of Grandfather Brenner's farm. His children, twin girls Margaret and Merriam, and two boys, Paul and Robert, would become an important part of my life. It was a real thrill when Hope and I were allotted an hour or two of playtime at the Tice Brenner farm. Hide and seek was a favorite game. Sometimes we would explore the farm. In the winter, we would walk the mile and a half to country school together.

Paul loved dairy cows and was destined to become a dairy farmer. He hated school and became a high school dropout. Our friendship continued throughout his life. During my law school days, he would come to Lincoln occasionally. A time or two, we would double date. Before and during the time I was Governor, Paul was a frequent visitor to our home in Lincoln. He and his wife were fond of my wife and would frequently ask her for advice.

For a year or two, while attending college, Robert lived with us. He had a lovely voice and was a member of the Kansas State Glee Club.

Before leaving Colorado, my closest relative friends were twin cousins, Berniece and Bernita Morrison, and their sister who was known as "Bob." On moving to the farm near Manhattan, my closest relative friends were also twins, Margaret and Merriam Brenner. Both Margaret and Merriam were short, human dynamos, full of life. For Merriam, school, including college, was but a means to getting a teaching job, earning money, and marrying a farm boy from Larned.

Merriam made me a needed loan when I was in law school.

Well organized, serious, and possessing a cynical sense of humor she inherited from her dad, Margaret had a thirst for knowledge, accomplishment, career, and family. We were together frequently during our college years. Before her death, Margaret compiled a book entitled Family Archives which is a treasure. The sacrifices, hard work, and dedication she exhibited during her college days and thereafter, and her experiences in New York and Baltimore as a young professional are a blueprint for every young American that you can reach the top if you are so motivated. While serving as home agent in Elko, Nevada, she met and married Henry Garat, a member of a prominent Nevada ranch family. They had three girls who never experienced their mother's type of privation, but they have all made a substantial contribution to this nation's educational and cultural life. Margaret, Merriam, Paul, and Robert were all my childhood role models on Wildcat Creek.

After the birth of a fifth child, Francis, the Tice Brenner family moved thirty miles north to a farm near Waterville. Our contacts were far less frequent but continued through the years with my visits to the farm, which included helping with the annual wheat harvest.

On this Wildcat Creek farm, I was introduced to the beginning of life. Cows gave birth to calves, chickens hatched from eggs, and my Aunt Maude, Uncle Tice's wife, grew heavy with child which resulted in a new cousin named Francis. I had watched animals copulate which resulted in this new life and marveled at the mystery of it all.

I was also introduced to accidental death. Grandfather had hauled rock to build a ford across the creek which would facilitate moving farm machinery to the land on the south side. The water then cut a deep hole in the creek below the ford. On the Fourth of July, many townspeople would escape the heat of the city to let their kids enjoy the cool water of Wildcat Creek. A clothing store in Manhattan was owned by a family named Manschart. The parents had two children, a boy about my age and a daughter some two years younger. On Independence Day, 1914, the Manscharts asked permission to use the creek on our land. Several hours later, their seven-year-old girl came to the house and reported that she thought her father, mother, and brother had drowned. We rushed to the creek and discovered people in the water attempting to recover the victims. One body was on the bank receiving artificial respiration to no avail. That was when I was conscious of witnessing death for the first time.

My grandmother, Charlotte Brenner, introduced me to the social sciences, political life, and the Bible. By the light of a kerosene lamp, she put her stamp upon my life forever. She told me about our country, political parties, the Bible, and the Methodist Church. She believed that public service was to be respected. She told me that in our country one great political issue divided the country: free

Frank B. Morrison (5 years old) with sister Eva Hope Morrison
Brush, Colorado, 1910

trade versus protective tariff. Even though she and her husband were farmers, she felt that young American industry must be protected to grow and survive by the nation levying a tax on imports. This was the Republican doctrine. She said that Democrats stood for free trade, which would destroy our young industries.

She told me about God and how he had revealed himself to us through the King James version of the Bible. She sat me down each night and had me read to her a chapter from the Bible. This had a profound effect on my ability to read as well as teaching me Hebrew history and the origin of the Jewish and Christian traditions.

My first dim memory of my grandmother, Charlotte Smith Brenner, hardly rises to the realm of consciousness. It seems more like a dream. My mother took my sister, Hope, and me back to Manhattan in 1907 after my father's death for a visit with her parents. Missing our father, grandmother told me he went to live with Jesus. I could never understand why he would leave me to go and live with someone else.

My next contact with Grandmother Brenner was in 1911 when Hope and I were sent to live with her. At that time, she was 61. She, I, and everyone else at that time regarded her as an old woman. Her skirts drug on the ground. She wore an apron which she folded up each day to hold grain as she went out to feed the chickens. I regard my own children, who are about her age, as young. In today's world, women stay young much longer. Grandmother Brenner could not imagine responsible women dancing or making a public display of their bodies. I remember one time we were given free tickets to the Barnum and Bailey Circus because she permitted circus advertising on our barn. The circus included the proverbial leg show. She could not believe these were actually women. She contended that they were men dressed up as women. Notwithstanding all of this, she was a natural-born teacher who wanted to educate me to become a Methodist Bishop which, to her, was the most important post in the world. For her, there was the well-known heavenly trinity. An earthly trinity consisted of the U.S. government, the Methodist Church, and the Republican Party. I have often wondered what this lady would have thought and done had she lived in the latter part of the 20th century.

Every Sunday, we would hitch the horses to the carriage and journey to the Methodist Episcopal Church in Manhattan. In Sunday School my family faith was fortified with the fundamentalist interpretation of the origin of the earth, life, and man himself. I never doubted that God created the earth in six days. After creating animal and plant life, he took up some dust and made man in his own image, then laid him down, took out a rib, and created woman. My later study of science caused me to question these details of creation, but my basic faith in a purpose in life, the spiritual nature of existence, and the awesomeness of the universe has never left my conscious existence.

On a beautiful December snow-covered night they loaded my ill grandmother into the buggy. I hitched my sled to the back of the buggy, and we took grandmother to the hospital from which she never returned. This was my first conscious experience of death in the family. My grandmother had left me to join her parents and her Lord in a place called Heaven. Her body, however, was buried in Sunset Cemetery, a beautiful spot on the west edge of the city. My grief was relieved when I went to church and repeated the Apostles Creed which, among many things, states, "I believe in the resurrection of the body." As a child, I never doubted that someday I would meet my beloved grandmother in that place called Heaven and that her embalmed body would rise from that grave in Sunset Cemetery to meet me on those golden streets where we would live in eternal bliss. I would also be reunited with my father forever. The faith of a little child was created and nourished by this lady who taught me how to read "God's Word."

In Sunday School I met or saw kids who were to become prominent in American life. James Price was to become a distinguished lawyer, president of two major universities and dean of two different American law schools.

It was also in Sunday School that I first saw a boy in knickerbockers, the son of our newspaper publisher, Fred Seaton. Fred later became an American statesman, President of the Young Republicans of the United States, an officer in Alf Landon's presidential campaign, a member of the Nebraska Legislature, publisher of the Hastings *Tribune,* and Secretary of the Interior in the Eisenhower administration. He was my opponent for the governorship of Nebraska in the 1962 election.

When I first met him, Fred was a visitor from the Episcopal Sunday School. Even at that time, he had the immaculate dress for which he was famous. The customary dress for boys in this period included knee-length knickerbockers. Their fundamentalist religion obviously did not hamper their earthly success.

In country school, two miles from home by road, or one and one-half miles cutting through fields, I learned reading, writing, and arithmetic taught to the tune of a dedicated teacher. I was taught to recite memorized scripts before our parents on Parents Day.

The schoolhouse, which still stands, was built of limestone and, during my tenure, was enlarged into two rooms with some sixty students and two teachers. The Kansas State University football stadium is now located about one-half mile from this schoolhouse which today is part of the Manhattan school system.

We walked to school regardless of weather. I remember one winter day the snow was close to a foot deep, the wind was in the north, and the temperature about ten degrees below zero. When we arrived at school, my cousin Robert's ears were frozen and he was in a stupor. My own ears were frozen but soon thawed out. The school had become a temporary first-aid station. In those days, school was never canceled because of weather. Weather was just one of those things you learned to live with. This conformed to my mother's ethic of self-determination. Contrary to today's custom, I was told that if I was punished by the teacher for misbehavior that I would be whipped again when I returned home. The teacher was to be respected and obeyed at school.

An indispensable part of my education on the farm was imparted by my grandmother's sister, Aunt Risa. She was a widow who lived with my grandparents after her husband's death. A half-blind retired school teacher, she spun yarns and told stories by the hour to my sister and me. This was sheer entertainment but taught me a valuable lesson. We must distinguish between fiction and fact if we are to make wise decisions. Judgment, based on fantasy and perception rather than truth, can be disastrous.

In the winter of 1915-16, my grandfather, Jacob, contracted what he thought was kidney disease. He was having trouble urinating, so he prescribed for himself Doan's Little Kidney Pills. The result was disastrous. One night, his urine was completely shut off and I have never seen a human being in such pain. A family doctor who made house calls in the country twenty-four hours a day was called. He said my grandfather had cancer. We harnessed the horse and headed for the hospital where it was discovered his enlarged prostate gland was the culprit. To relieve his pain, the doctor ran a knife through his abdomen and into his bladder. Later, they removed the prostate surgically, but the original cut never healed and became infected. He lived three years as an invalid with my mother periodically catheterizing and otherwise caring for him in addition to her other duties. This was my first introduction to severe human pain and helplessness.

Water for the farm was supplied by an open well about fifteen feet deep. The water was raised from the bottom of the well by two oaken buckets attached to a chain which passed through a pulley wheel about eight feet above the ground. When one bucket was filled at the bottom of the well, it was raised and the other bucket was automatically lowered to the bottom of the well. This hand-drawn water furnished the needs of both animals and family.

Before we left the farm, I remember seeing on the road two strange machines: one became known to me as an automobile and the other was a motorcycle. I never dreamed that either I, my sister, or our family would ever be able to afford one of these.

My mother had moved in with her father, Jacob Brenner, in 1912 so she could take care of him. By 1916, it was obvious this crippled Civil War veteran, now in his seventies, was no longer able to operate his farm. The farm, which grew corn, alfalfa, apples, and vegetables, was to pass out of his life forever.

Jacob Brenner was the only male figure in my life during this time of my youth. He had offered to give his life to preserve the political unity of his country and to end human slavery. My vivid memory of his milking a cow with only one finger and a thumb on his right hand was the miracle of my childhood. That crippled hand would be, for me, the indelible brand of the nobility of the American political system.

We sold my beloved animals and moved to town.

---

6 In 1912 Republican William Howard Taft was president. Former president Theodore Roosevelt tried to win the Republican nomination but Taft had a firm grip on the party machinery. When Roosevelt failed to win the nomination, he became the nominee of a third party, the U. S. Progressive Party. This was popularly known as the Bull Moose Party, referring to Roosevelt's determination and physical stamina. The Bull Moose Party platform backed conservation, women's suffrage, and the popular election of senators among other issues. In the general election, it received twenty-five percent of the popular vote. This fractious situation in the Republican Party resulted in the election of the Democratic nominee, Woodrow Wilson. Four years later, the Bull Moose Party ceased to exist and Roosevelt rejoined the Republican Party.

7 This was milk from which the cream had been removed.

Life at 914 Bluemont

My invalid grandfather, my mother, my sister Eva Hope (called Hope), and I moved into the large, two-story frame house at 914 Bluemont Avenue in Manhattan, Kansas in August 1916. It was located some four blocks east of the east gate to the campus of what was then known as Kansas State Agricultural College. Here this boy of eleven evolved into a man of twenty-two years.

In 1916, Manhattan was a beautiful little city of some seven thousand people nestled in a valley at the junction of the Blue and Kansas Rivers. This did not count the college, whose enrollment was approximately half that number. During the early evolution of the earth, this part of Kansas had once been a sea. The land was all under water and a thick layer of limestone came to the surface in places. Many farm fences were made of native stone harvested from the land. All of the college buildings were built of this stone quarried locally. The campus was surrounded by a limestone fence. A number of homes and commercial buildings were built of the same material.

Prior to the Civil War, Congress had repealed a part of the Missouri compromise by the passage of the Kansas-Nebraska Act which provided that Kansas and Nebraska would be admitted to the union as slave or free states by vote of the local people. Kansas then became a battleground between the slavery and anti-slavery people. Kansas became "bleeding Kansas." Our town was definitely anti-slavery. Manhattan of the early 20th century was as much New England in politics, religion, and culture as rural New England itself. It was White Anglo-Saxon Protestant Republican to the core. It was as puritanical in philosophy as the Puritans themselves. Prohibition was the law of the land. The sale of cigarettes was illegal. Dancing was prohibited in the public schools, including high school. The discipline of the Methodist Church, the dominant religion, even forbade the playing of cards. Universal human brotherhood was preached. There were no racial problems because there were practically no African-American, Native American, Southern European, or Asiatic peoples in town. A few Mexicans moved in to work the railroad beds of the Rock Island and Union Pacific Railroad which served the town. A number of blacks and foreign students attended the college, which reminded us that all of the world did not consist of WASPS. College fraternities were illegal at the college until 1914.

Pre-marital sex was an absolute no-no. Girls were not allowed to play inter-school athletics. Intramural women's basketball was allowed if the girls wore long, full bloomers and would stay in an allotted space on the floor to avoid physical contact. Prior to the time I graduated from college, I had never seen a bottle of alcoholic beverage, nor had I ever seen a student drink or become intoxicated. Over a period of the next eleven years, I remember only one murder and one rape case in the entire state of Kansas. Homes were almost never locked. It was into this social and cultural system I moved as a child of eleven years.

The day we moved to town, my lifestyle changed forever. The open well, the old oaken buckets, my friends - the cows, the horses, the pigs, and the chickens - were no longer a part of my life. Electricity replaced the kerosene lamps, a bath-room replaced the outdoor privy, and a glass milk bottle replaced the cow. Electricity was delivered to each room by a drop cord from the ceiling in the mid-dle of the room. There were no wall plugs or table lamps. One bathroom off the upstairs hall served the entire house. One hot-air furnace, which burned coal delivered through a basement window to a coal bin, replaced the coal-burning stoves we had used in each room of the farmhouse.

My mother went to work as storeroom keeper and purchasing agent for the Department of Home Economics at the college. Her $80 per month salary, plus grandfather's disability pension of $50 per month as a Civil War veteran, were not enough to pay the taxes, interest on the mortgage, medical bills, and living expenses, so she converted our home into a rooming house for female students at the college. One can imagine the traffic problems this caused in a one-bathroom house.

School was only five blocks from home which was quite a change from the rural school. I had an excellent teacher in the sixth grade. For the first time, I had a classmate who was the daughter of a celebrity. This was Wilma Searson, a cute little curly-haired girl, whose father wrote the Searson-Martin readers which were standard grade school reading textbooks in all Kansas schools as well as in other states. In this class was also Russell Thackery, who was later to become Milton Eisenhower's Chief Assistant when he was president at Kansas State University and then Executive Director of the Land Grant College Association of the United States. For the first time, I also had a classmate who would become a profession-al criminal. This was the first time in my life that I had known a boy who was to become a violent criminal. I remember when the teacher reported to the class sorrowfully that he had been jailed as a result of a burglary. One day we were standing in line at school when, without warning, this boy doubled his fist and hit me a stunning, violent blow to the back. This was my first brush with the violent, anti-social conduct which was to later become a major interest of my life.

1916 was a presidential year. Justice Charles Evans Hughes was nominated by the Republicans to challenge Woodrow Wilson. This was the first presidential election in which I took an interest. I remember arguing with a classmate by supporting the case of Hughes. I even lodged a five cent bet.

In history, I was taught that eight world powers ruled the world at that time. They were the British Empire which encompassed the world, France, Germany, Italy, Austria-Hungary, Russia, Japan, and the United States. The newest powers were Japan and the United States - Japan, as a result of its defeat of Russia in their war, and the United States as a result of its defeat of Spain in the Spanish-American War.

In 1914, the First World War was triggered by a Serbian national killing the Archduke of Austria. As a result, Germany, Austria-Hungary, and Bulgaria went to war against the British, France, Italy, Russia, Serbia, and Romania. I heard talk as a child about winning a war and I wondered how they determined the winner. Did they determine the winner by counting the dead bodies on each side?

Woodrow Wilson, in a close election, won re-election on the slogan that he "kept us out of war," meaning World War I. The next year, Wilson asked Congress for a declaration of war against the empires of Germany and Austria-Hungary, known as the central powers.

For the first time in my conscious existence, I heard people talking about a war which was then taking place in my lifetime. Prior to that time, I had only heard about wars in the past which were a part of history and not current.

As soon as school was out in the spring of 1917, it was time for a twelve-year-old boy to become gainfully employed. My half-sister, Hazel, and her husband, Orville, employed me at $12 per month to work on their farm near my mother's homestead. I elected to take the Rock Island train to Denver and the Union Pacific from Denver to a very small town near the farm called Snyder. The train was very late getting into Denver. The Union Pacific's only train that stopped at Snyder had left. It would be necessary for me to wait until the next day. I was a twelve-year-old boy in the giant Union Station in Denver. What would I do? I knew no one in Denver and had no place to stay overnight. I decided to take a Burlington train to Brush and hike the ten miles from Brush to the farm. I boarded the Burlington, got off at Brush, and started walking to the farm. Somewhere out of Brush, I encountered a man who was fixing a tire on one of those new-fangled automobiles. He told me he would drive me to my brother-in-law's place if I would wait until he fixed the tire. What a thrill! He drove me to the farm and we arrived in the middle of a wind, thunder, and sand storm. I had never seen that man before nor have I seen him since. I shall never forget that generosity from a total stranger.

My father's brother, Abraham Lincoln Morrison, lived on a farm near my sister who was pregnant and due to deliver in August. Uncle Linc, as we called him, found me barefoot one day and asked me why I did not wear work shoes. I said I could not afford them. The next day, he showed up with a new pair of work shoes for me. I will always remember this generosity from a relative.

Returning from a field one day driving a four-horse disc, I looked down at the jumping, churning discs below me as the horses ran full speed down the hill. If I fell in front, I would become mincemeat. So I made my life's first important decision: I opted for safety rather than adventure. I jumped off the disc. One horse was injured and the other crippled for life. The rest of the summer, my work was confined to helping with the chores and assisting my pregnant sister with the housework because I was too young to handle a disc.

Some two weeks before my sister was to deliver her baby, she was experiencing problems. I was ordered to sleep in the barn's hayloft in order to give my sister privacy. In 1917 twelve year old boys were too young to witness the ordeal of birth. I loved this experience in the hayloft. Eventually, one night my sister was taken to my uncle's house where my aunt delivered the baby. That baby, my niece, Doris, has always been near and dear to us.

Camp revival meetings were held each year. An evangelist was imported. He gave an impassioned sermon on the necessity to be saved from one's sins and to be born again as a prerequisite for entry into heaven. Hymns were sung until the atmosphere became quite ecstatic. At the proper time, all people who wanted to be saved from sin were asked to come forward while their friends prayed for them. The praying became intense. I came forward amid urgent pleas for my salvation, but I failed to receive any cataclysmic experience.

On my return to Manhattan I learned my first lesson on the unreliability of hearsay information. While walking from the railroad depot to 914 Bluemont, I encountered a boy acquaintance who informed me that my mother, who had been widowed for ten years, had given birth to a new baby. He insisted this was accurate. I was stunned and mortified. When I arrived home, I discovered my Aunt Edna, who lived in Chicago, was in an upstairs bedroom with a brand new baby boy named Paul Snyder. She had come to Manhattan to have her baby born in our home. This was a great relief. Little did I know at the time the tremendous impact this young mother would have on my life.

I soon entered the seventh grade, my first year in junior high school. My employment consisted of hawking newspapers on the street and acquiring a paper route. The First World War was on. Everyone was on a great mission to make the world safe for democracy and to end all war for the future. The schools and churches were helping work people into a frenzy. The teaching of German in the schools was outlawed. A picture show was produced called the "Kaiser, Beast of Berlin." I heard a British and French officer speak at church services telling how the German soldiers were committing acts of atrocity such as cutting off women's breasts and hitting babies' heads over rocks. At school, we were taught songs such as "The Yanks are Coming," "Over High Garden Walls, a Soldier Boy Calls," and "Good-bye Ma, Good-bye Pa, Good-bye Mule with Your Old Hee Haw, I may not know what this war's about, but I bet by gosh, I will soon find out."

Camp Funston was built next to Fort Riley, about sixteen miles out of town. The city was flooded with soldiers. The church converted its annex into a soldier barracks. The commanding general of Camp Funston was a battle-scarred, old veteran of the Spanish-American war named Leonard Wood. He became my boyhood hero. In my eyes, he was leading the troops to end the forces of evil in the world. The commander in chief of this great crusade was President Woodrow Wilson, son of a Presbyterian minister, himself a great scholar, historian, political idealist, and former president of Princeton University. In retrospect, I learned that when idealism and fantasy are divorced from reality in the formulation of public policy, the result is costly. The real lesson was: you can never end all war by engaging in war. No generation can ever make the world safe for following generations. As I look at the world today, I wonder how many have learned this lesson.

When thirteen-year-old eighth grader, Frank Brenner Morrison, heard of the Armistice which ended World War I, the most important thing on his mind was to celebrate. He descended on the principal's office with a gang of other kids to demand a holiday. As we celebrated, these junior high kids, as well as the rest of the world, were totally unconscious of the fact that this was but a prelude to the Treaty of Versailles where the lust for power would carve up central Europe, exact humiliating and burdensome damages on the German people, and lay the groundwork for hate, revenge, and retaliation. This would then spawn the Nazi Party, the rise of Adolph Hitler, and the creation of one of the most cruel, bloody, and dangerous dictatorships in human history. Woodrow Wilson's dream of a League of Nations to end all war had been shattered by blind parochialism at home and the human lust for power and nationalistic expansion abroad. This combination eventually built the cross which threatened to crucify civilization.

The first winter of the war, I had a paper route and hawked newspapers on the street screaming exciting headlines.

Aggieville was a business district adjoining the college campus. There was a bookstore and a variety store. The largest building contained a restaurant with soda fountain and a grocery store on the ground floor and a dance hall on the second floor. This was the prohibition era where the sale of alcoholic beverages was illegal. Each Saturday night, the college kids would hold a dance after imbibing soft drinks and ice cream at the soda fountain. Occasionally, organizations such as the Knights of Columbus would hold a dance there.

In this setting, junior high kid, Frank Morrison, obtained the job as janitor for the dance hall. My Methodist ban on dancing must give way to the necessity of supplementing the family income. After each dance, I was supposed to sprinkle sweeping compound over the dance floor, then sweep with a broom, followed by pushing over the floor an instrument which resembled a small blanket wrapped around a plank with a handle attached. It was my duty to empty all ashtrays. Even though the sale of cigarettes was illegal, college kids obtained them from tobacco bootleggers. The only evidence that I encountered of alcohol use was after a Knights of Columbus dance. One guest became drunk and caused an environmental problem. During my year as janitor, this was the only evidence of alcohol I ever encountered.

When college vacation began in June, I abandoned the janitor's job and became a field worker at the college ag station. My job was to hoe weeds. One of my classmates, Rushton Countelyou, was a co-worker. Rushton was a sophisticate and later a member of our high school debate team. His father was a member of the college faculty. His mother was the daughter of the Rushton who founded the world famous food company with a creamery in Fairmont, Nebraska. Rushton loved to engage me in philosophical discussions calling into question my fundamentalist religious beliefs. After finishing college, Rushton, at one time, became treasurer of Fairmont Foods and then a member of the faculty at Bellevue College in Nebraska.

One morning in late August, 1919, while I was so employed, I visited my grandfather's bedside. This Civil War veteran with the crippled hand, who had offered his life to save American political unity, was dying. The deathly blue was starting in his hands, and he was peacefully ending the conscious experience of life on earth. When I returned from work that night, his bedroom was empty. The undertaker had come and removed his body. That mangled hand will never die. It has branded itself on my conscious being forever. For me, it will always be the symbol of sacrifices made to preserve the American political system.

The emotional impact of my grandfather's death converted an honor student into a failure. I flunked two courses in the ninth and tenth grades and was forced to retake a final exam in a third. It was not until eleventh grade that the failed student was again returned to the honor roll.

The summer of 1920 was historic. The Republican convention deadlocked between my hero, General Wood, Governor Lowden of Illinois, and Senator

Hiram Johnson of California. It resulted in the nomination of Warren Harding, an unknown, in what became known as a smoke-filled room. The Democrats nominated a newspaper man from Ohio, James Cox. Harding was elected.

I had spent my summer working in the wheat country of western Kansas south of Colby. The following winter, my grandfather's love of the garden got the best of me. During the last years of his life, my grandfather had been mobile enough to get me involved in a garden business on vacant lots near the house. Tomatoes were our mainstay. I loved to grow tomatoes. I learned how to build a hotbed to start the plants in the backyard. This led me into a new business. A man named Collins had a glass greenhouse back of his home some two blocks west of us. I went to see him about buying some glass for my hotbed. He ended up selling me the greenhouse, taking my promissory note for payment, and the fifteen-year-old boy was in the greenhouse business.

I moved it into the backyard at 914 Bluemont. My specialty was growing tomato plants by the thousands for both wholesale and retail markets. In addition, I grew cabbage and aster plants. In the area of flowers, I grew sweet peas. I installed my own furnace and heating system and built a workshop at the end of the greenhouse. One might expect this commercial activity would discourage my schooling, but the opposite was true.

The city of Manhattan built its only public high school on the south side of Poyntz Avenue in the 900 block. This beautiful, functional building was built of native Kansas limestone. The only change after eighty years of use is that it is now used as a junior high or middle school. In this building I learned that teaching is the most important of all professions. It determines the quality of all others, including that of parenting and statesmanship. No teacher in my first two years of high school inspired or motivated me. That all changed in my junior year when my teachers did inspire and motivate me. I became determined to enlarge the perimeters of my consciousness and play a more important role in the world around me.

During my fifteenth year of life, I had grown fast, slim, and tall. All of this only exaggerated my poor coordination. I was ill suited for interschool athletic competition. My physical exercise was limited to my greenhouse work, walking to school, being an active Boy Scout, and intramural basketball.

I loved my greenhouse and all growing things, but something happened in my junior year in high school that would dictate my profession. I took a course in economics taught by the high school principal who had a law degree. He was also the high school debate coach. In those days, this was an important school activity. One day after class, he demanded to know why I was not out for debate. I gave three no-good reasons. First, I did not think I would be good and I was bashful.

Second, I had not tried out. Third, he already had his debate team. Regardless of my reasons, or maybe because of them, he demanded that I report for debate. This teacher changed my life forever. I loved debate, the spoken word, the clash of ideas, and the stage. The debate of important public policy convinced me to become a lawyer and spend my life in pursuit of human justice. From then on, my greenhouse was only a tool to help finance my education; it was not a permanent business. My interest in academics skyrocketed. I was converted from a failure to an honor student. I discovered that one teacher can change a student's life forever.

The short, pudgy lawyer, teacher, administrator, and debate coach was not the only teacher in high school who inspired me. There was a quiet, humble woman who taught history. I have never forgotten the opening lines of the Declaration of Independence. Basic human rights such as life, liberty, and the pursuit of happiness flowed from our Creator and the purpose of government was to protect, not violate them. The dedication of our founding fathers became real and meaningful. The Constitution and Lincoln's Gettysburg Address became sacred to me.

My English teacher introduced me to Keats, Shelley, Wordsworth, Dickens, and Shakespeare. Their rhetoric and their world became my world. I was awed by Shakespeare's comprehension of life and human conduct. My English teacher also taught me to learn a poem by Tennyson that gave botany a new meaning:

> *"Flower in the crannied wall,*
> *I pluck you out of the crannies,*
> *I hold you here, root and all, in my hand,*
> *Little flower - but if I could understand*
> *What you are, root and all, and all in all,*
> *I should know what God and man is."*[8]

My, how all this enriched my own life!

My botany teacher forever branded me with curiosity to discover how chlorophyl works to manufacture sugar, the basis of all food. That mystery still remains unsolved. What a challenge!

My physics teacher pulled back the curtain on the secret powers of nature. The nucleus, gravity, atom, sound waves, electricity, magnetism, light, and a host of other natural phenomena, became the fascinating mysteries of the cosmos to explore.

In Manhattan High School, I learned what many educators have never learned: The greatest service a teacher can perform is to uncork the bottled-up appetite of the student to enhance the breadth and quality of his or her own consciousness of the world, its excitement, meaning, and potential. The dominant purpose of my life then was to try and comprehend the meaning of it all. I can never repay my debt to Manhattan High School.

I learned in my middle teens that my junior high geography knowledge that Minnesota was the number one wheat-producing state was obsolete. Kansas had now replaced Minnesota as the leading wheat producer. At that time in eastern Kansas, a horse-drawn binder cut the wheat and bound it into bundles which were tied with binder twine. The bundles were then discharged onto the ground where they were picked up by hand and placed in shocks. Later, they were either hauled to stacks or to a threshing machine which separated the grain from the straw.

Western Kansas was almost one gigantic wheat field. Wheat fields were much larger than in eastern Kansas. Combines, which cut and threshed the wheat at one time, were rare. I had not seen one. The predominant way to harvest wheat in western Kansas was by heading. A header was a large horse-drawn machine with a long sickle bar which cut the wheat and delivered it to a rolling canvas, which elevated it to a horse-drawn wagon called a header barge. Here a man with a pitchfork would spread the straw containing the wheat heads until the barge was full. Another barge would move into place. The first barge would then deliver its cargo to a stack. Later, a threshing machine would drop by and the wheat from the stack was delivered to the machine which would separate the grain from the straw.

Corn picking machines were not yet invented. All corn was picked by hand.

Two of the women students who roomed with my mother had a brother, Earl Howard, who managed their family wheat farm south of Colby, Kansas. During my fifteenth, seventeenth, and eighteenth years, while my greenhouse was idle in the summer, I would travel to the Howard farm, work in the wheat harvest, and remain thereafter to prepare the ground for seeding in the fall. Unlike the itinerant harvest hands who only helped with the wheat harvest, I would do chores, such as milking the cows, after returning from the field. All of us would participate in harnessing and unharnessing the horses.

Earl Howard and his family practiced family devotions. Earl would read a chapter from the Bible each morning before work. The family members would then descend to their knees and Earl would lead the prayer for the day. Most of the harvest hands would join in the devotions. There were normally three of them besides Earl, his family, and myself.

I would return to Manhattan and school late in August after a hard summer's work.

As my mind flashes back to my high school days I think of the beautiful, charming girls, but I was far too bashful, timid, and tight to ask them for a date. There was Helen King, daughter of the college chemistry department head. She grew up, went out to Norton to teach, and married the golf pro. Her sister, Kathryn, married Paul Chappell who left for West Point and an army career. Helen's closest friend was Helen Eaken who married Milton Eisenhower, President Eisenhower's youngest brother. She died far too soon while Milton was president of Pennsylvania State University. The chapel at Penn State is her memorial.

It is strange the things I remember. One day I overheard some of the girls gossiping about the daring low-cut dresses the Tri Delt girls from across the street were wearing to a college function. I thought I might like to have seen this.

One special girl in my class impressed me. Her name was Jessie Atkins. She had the grace of a swan, the beauty of a movie actress, and a low, soft voice which landed her the lead in the senior class play. I had tried out for a part in this play, but because of a case of barber's itch, which disfigured my face, I was made business manager. In addition to seeing her in class, this gave me an opportunity to be with this angel from paradise in play rehearsals.

It is strange that none of my high school friends and acquaintances, no matter how much I admired them, became lifelong friends. Intramural basketball, the Boy Scouts, Sunday school, Epworth League,[9] debate, and the Forensic Club[10] constituted the source of all of my social life.

Our school idol was a boy named "Chilie" Cochran. "Chilie" had a ruddy complexion and auburn hair, which accounted for his nickname. He was a football and basketball star in high school and a football star at K-State. He married Merl Broberg, Jessie Atkins' best friend, and went on to become assistant football coach at Indiana University.

Two boys from my Sunday school class I admired a great deal. One, the son of a banker who was convicted of embezzlement, was James Pratt. He went on to become a professional accountant. The other was James Price. He had a beautiful baritone voice, was on our debate squad, and had the lead in the senior play. He was on both the basketball and football teams, and was a tennis and golf player. He graduated with honors and was granted a scholarship to Swarthmore. The next year, he became student body president of the University Afloat, sponsored by City College of New York. His last two years, he returned to K-State where he debated and played football. After college, he obtained a law degree from Stanford, had a career as dean of the law schools at Washburn and Denver University. He was University President at Emporia State and Denver University, retiring to practice law in southern California.

Compared to my friends, James Pratt, the banker's son, and James Price, the only son of a history professor at K-State, I was a fatherless, poor boy. I shall never forget the time I showed up in Sunday school with my green plaid $15 suit from Montgomery Wards, while both of them appeared in $30 beautiful suits.

My green house and my high school graduation gown.

My friend, Forrest Whan from the debate team, had a career in speech on the faculty at Iowa State and Wichita University. Rushton Cortelyou from the debate team inherited wealth which probably hampered his professional development.

My high school career ended, and I was ready for college. The State of Kansas had two law schools, one at the University of Kansas in Lawrence, the other at Washburn in Topeka. They, like most law schools, required at least two years of college before admission. What should be my next step? Mother insisted I have a college degree before going to law school. This appealed to me, for I could teach to earn money with which to finance my law education. It was logical to do my college work at K-State, then known as the Kansas State Agricultural College. I could stay at home, operate my greenhouse, and prepare myself for law school.

Kansas State placed a great deal of emphasis on the natural sciences. Ten hours of inorganic chemistry and eight hours of physics were required courses. My interest was primarily in the social sciences, and I took many courses in this field, but in later life, I was thankful for the time I spent in chemistry and physics. It gave me a far better understanding of the physical world around me. This not only made me a better citizen, but I later found it useful in the trial of lawsuits.

In freshman chemistry class, I met Lawrence Youngman, who was the first classmate to become my friend for life. We called him Doc because his father was a doctor in Harveyville, Kansas. My first year, I did not pledge a fraternity but longed to become a part of the social life. Kansas State had one of the most ridiculous hazing customs you could imagine. Fraternity hazing dominated the whole campus. All freshmen were required to wear green skull caps. If a freshman was found not wearing his cap at a football game, he was taken to the side of the field and placed on a blanket, which was quickly tightened, propelling the freshman many feet into the air. If a freshman was found on the street without his cap, he was forced to run down the middle of the street with blocks of upper classmen wielding wooden paddles to apply to the victim's rear end. All of this ridiculous activity was less dangerous than today's drunken orgies.

My urge to become a part of college social life led me to discard the Methodist doctrine against dancing and playing cards. I took dancing lessons, started to date, and learned to play bridge.

I wanted to polish my skills as a debater, extemporaneous speaker, and orator. I not only liked these activities, but they prepared me to become a trial lawyer. At that time, K-State had a system of literary societies with such names as Athenian, Ionian, Hamilton, Webster etc. They met on the campus every Saturday night. Each member was responsible for at least one program a year and was required to speak before the society. This was a great educational tool, but started to evaporate during my years in college in view of the trend to do what feels good, not what develops your brain.

Kansas State had a top military program. Close order drill, together with courses in military science and tactics, were required the first two years. The second two were optional. In the second two, you became an officer in the cadet corps, wore a tailor-made officer's uniform, and were paid a small monthly salary. I became a student infantry cadet for four years. On graduation, I was commissioned a second lieutenant in the United States Infantry Reserves.

My first year of college passed all too soon. My greenhouse stood dormant in the summer so I decided not to spend my summers in the western Kansas wheat fields, south of Colby, but to try my skills at house-to-house salesmanship. I decided to sell farm books to farmers. I attended classes to learn how to sell these much needed reference books. At that time, I was driving my hand-cranked Model T Ford. When school was out, I invited two of my college friends, Heath and Ferris, to ride with me to southeast Minnesota, disperse, and start selling farm books. Heath and I were not successful. Ferris was. Heath discovered a set of tools to aid farm wives in their canning operations. All farm women in Iowa and Minnesota canned vegetables and fruit for winter use. Heath and I were an instant success in northeast Iowa selling farm women on this useful commodity. As fall approached, the three of us decided to take a vacation to Chicago where both Ferris and I had relatives.

My mother's sister, Flora Edna Brenner Snyder, was an attractive, intelligent graduate of K-State in Home Economics. She had fallen in love with a young man named M. J. Snyder. He was from a town where she was teaching. They were married on the farm where she had sung for my mother's wedding years before. Afterward, they moved to Chicago where her husband was employed. When I visited them in late August of 1924, he was in bed dying from an incurable kidney disease called nephritis. He had been hospitalized for weeks. The medical and hospital bills had exhausted their resources. They had three children: Paul, age 6; Charlotte, age 4; and Bill, age 1. The family decided I should stay out of school and take charge of the house. My cousin, Margaret, was drafted to come and do the cooking and keep house so that my aunt could spend time with her husband in Cook County Hospital until he died. My aunt and her family lived in Oak Park, a nice suburb west of Chicago. It was necessary to find employment so I obtained a job as an ironworker's assistant on rebuilding the Palmer House in downtown Chicago. I traveled back and forth on the "el" (short for elevated). My greenhouse being dormant in the fall, I had no problem with the Chicago living.

M. J. Snyder, father of three and husband of my mother's sister, was only thirty-three when he died in Cook County Hospital in October. My mother and sister Hope had stayed with them to help during the summer but it was necessary for my sister to go back to school and for mother to return to her job at K-State. Mother took the oldest Snyder child, Paul, with her so that he could enter first grade in Manhattan. I quit my job. M. J.'s body was placed in a casket. Margaret, my aunt Edna, Charlotte, Bill, and I accompanied the body on a train back to Manhattan. Aunt Edna and the children moved in with us and she obtained a job in a bookstore in downtown Manhattan. Margaret went back to her parents and stayed out of school the rest of the semester. I went back to college determined to make up the lost time.

My second year of college proved to be very interesting. My friend and co-worker in house-to-house sales, Senn Heath, interested me in pledging his local fraternity, Kappa Phi Alpha, based on the fact that it had petitioned the prestigious Sigma Chi national for a chapter. The housemother was a crippled lady who needed help to walk, but she was a dictator on etiquette. Men seated women at the table. Table manners must be strictly adhered to. A man always kept his date to the right, except when walking on the sidewalk where he must protect the lady by walking on the street side. A man must tip his hat to all ladies he passed on the street. To me, it is a tragedy that we have lost some of this respect and elegance in life.

Sigma Chi declined our petition because of a veto by KU which had the only Sigma Chi chapter in the state. We then merged with another local fraternity, Alpha Sigma Psi. I was appointed chairman of a committee to select another national fraternity to be petitioned. After some research I recommended Tau Kappa Epsilon. The Committee accepted my recommendation. This was 1927. Alpha Lambda Chapter of Tau Kappa Epsilon at Kansas State University was granted but not installed until 1931 when I was a senior in law school at the University of Nebraska. I was therefore never a member of a national social fraternity during my Kansas State college days.

Owning the only transportation in the family, I became a chauffeur. My aunt was employed at the Endicott Bookstore downtown. I remember that one morning when I was taking my aunt to work, I collided with a streetcar at an intersection, which resulted in knocking a window out of the streetcar. My aunt became my aggressive defender in an attempt by the streetcar to force me to pay for the damage. She was successful.

This was the year I became engaged in intercollegiate debate, represented by the Athenian Literary Society in its annual intersociety contest. I won with an oration entitled "Public Opinion and World Peace." This was the start of my dedication to substituting reason for war.

By 1923, Henry Ford had made automobiles commonplace. My uncle Ed Morrison had died in Wheatland, Wyoming, and my sister Hope and I each inherited $1,000. I asked my mother to invest between $300 and $400 in a brand new Ford Model T touring car. This vehicle was an open, two-seater without batteries. It had a crank in front attached to a magnetto which generated electricity

Infantry Lieutenant, Frank Brenner Morrison

for the spark plugs. This crank took a good strong man to operate. On a cold winter morning, it might be necessary to pour hot water over the mechanism to start it even with prolonged cranking. This was the vehicle I used to transport family, friends, and my aunt.

At the end of my second year in college, I elected to replace the old shingles on the south side of our house with new ones and do some painting. This occupied most of the summer vacation. The last month, I decided to attend a camp owned and operated by the YMCA and the YWCA in the mountains outside of Estes Park, Colorado. Even though I was a native of that state, I had never been in the mountains. I was to make this trip in my Model T at the high speed of twenty miles per hour over dirt roads. My passengers were to be two YW girl students and my mother, who would visit Colorado relatives.

I shall never forget my first entrance into Big Thompson Canyon. I was awestruck by the vast expanse of stone reaching to a clear blue sky, a canyon carved by millions of years of slow erosion of the Big Thompson's waters. What a gift from my creator to see these things and hear the internal roar of the river.

Some generous person had donated a beautiful tract of land outside Estes Park near the foot of Long's Peak for the use of the YM and YW. It was equipped with modern meeting, eating, and housing facilities. This was a new conscious experience for the kid from Wildcat Creek. I totally enjoyed meeting, hiking, playing, singing, and studying with other students from all over America.

One day, some boy and girl friends from Kansas State decided to spend the day climbing Long's Peak, the mountain my mother had viewed from afar to renew her strength after my father's death. I drove the car as far as possible and then struck out for the "boulder field." By the time we were half through the boulder field, the girls gave out even though one of them was an athlete, later head of athletics at William Woods College. The boys and I continued on up to the top of this great mountain. My appreciation of the greatness of creation exploded. We picked the girls up on our way back through the boulder field. On this trip to and from Colorado, we drove all night. I remember getting so sleepy on the way back that I kept slapping my face to stay awake.

I had become active in the YMCA, whose executive director at K-State was an old football player from Colgate named Holtz. I had taken notice of a tall, green-eyed, blond, attractive girl in the crowd of students that gathered in Anderson Hall for a little recreation. At that time, I had never acquired the ability to approach and introduce myself to strangers, an ability for which I became famous in later life. It was sometime later that I attended a picnic in the country sponsored by the YM and YW. By some miracle, I found the courage to invite this girl to ride back to town with me. After depositing her at the Tri-Delt sorority house, I discovered she had left her hat in my car. The next day, I called and made

My Model T and friends

arrangements to return it. This was the start of a romance with Ruth Barnhisel that lasted the rest of my college career at Kansas State.

Near the end of the year, I was elected as a delegate to the Pi Kappa Delta honorary forensic fraternity convention in Estes Park. This took place in March and gave me an opportunity to be in the mountains when it snowed a little each day, converting the mountains into an artist's and skier's paradise. My friend on the debate squad, Frank Glick, later became a well-known scholar who founded the School of Social Service at the University of Nebraska. Ruth and I planned to get married sometime in the future.

After my junior year I attended summer ROTC training camp at Fort Snelling, Minnesota. Cadets from all over this part of the United States trained there. On one occasion, we had a full dress parade in honor of the Crown Prince of Sweden who stood in the reviewing stand. We studied advanced military science and tactics and were allowed some free time.

I had taken my Model T to Minnesota so I invited some of my friends to take a trip with me to Lake Superior, Hibbing, and Canada over the Fourth of July weekend. We witnessed the trains from the iron ore country unloading their cargo onto ships at Duluth. We went on to International Falls and crossed into Canada. We noticed the quiet; no noise or celebration existed across the border in Canada. What a difference a political line makes in what people deem important.

Upon completion of my tour of duty at Fort Snelling, I took my Model T and headed south for Columbus Junction, Iowa. My half-sister, Hazel, for whom I worked at age twelve in Colorado, now lived there. I had over a month left of my summer vacation. My brother-in-law, Orville, owned a tomato canning factory and put me to work immediately. He handed me a scoop shovel and asked me to help him unload a railroad car of coal into the fuel bin at the factory. I had no idea a railroad car held so much coal. It certainly accelerated my ambition to become a teacher and a lawyer. After a season's supply of coal was in the bin, I picked tomatoes and did other work around the factory until it was time to return to Manhattan for my senior year in college. My chief relief from that month of hard factory work was my daily letter from Ruth.

My senior year in college was eventful. This was the year I became involved in student politics. I attended school with Aunt Edna who was working on her master's degree in home economics. I was put in charge of a debate team to engage the University of Nebraska in Lincoln, Creighton in Omaha, and South Dakota in Vermillion. At home we debated some good universities like Northwestern. One of our subjects was Col. Mitchell's program for making the Air Force a separate department in the defense department. It was on my trip to Nebraska and South Dakota on this debate trip where I would meet people who were to play a role later in my life.

Evert "Bud" Hunt, a member of the University of Nebraska debate team, was to become a classmate in law school, my friend, and financial adviser when I was Governor and thereafter. Also, on the University of Nebraska team was David Fellman, who would debate with me at Nebraska. He had one of the finest minds I have ever known. After trying and not liking law school, he majored in political science, joined the faculty at Wisconsin University in Madison, and became President of the American Association of University Professors.

At Creighton, I met Frank Fogarty, debate coach, who later became head of the Chamber of Commerce in Omaha and manager of WOW-TV. The lead debater was Jim Fitzgerald, who would become County Attorney in Omaha.

In addition to operating my greenhouse, I engaged in the business of selling students' books on a commission. I also developed a desk blotter for students containing advertising by local merchants. I should never have accepted these blotters for they contained many typographical errors. They were printed by Fay Seaton, editor and father of my friend, Fred Seaton. I was far too soft and refused to demand a discount.

This was the year I would plunge into student politics. On the campus was one of the most dynamic and able young women I have ever known, Alice Nichols from Liberal, Kansas. Only early death while serving as editor of a leading New York newspaper kept her from becoming a real giant in journalism.

Student elections for class officers had been controlled by a small group of fraternities and sororities. Alice, in 1926, had surrounded herself with some friends

College days

to put a stop to this monopoly by organizing a new party called the Theodoric, named for the progressive Republican President, Teddy Roosevelt.

My girlfriend, Ruth Barnhisel, in addition to being a full-time student, was secretary to the manager of the college cafeteria. Her Tri Delt Sorority was one of the inside powerful cliques. She was their nominee for treasurer of the junior class.

Alice, who was a Chi Omega, decided to organize the independents and the balance of the Greeks into her Theodoric Party. She included, as a leader in her group, one of my friends, Lawrence Youngman. The insiders had nominated one of my closest friends, Paul Axtell, assistant librarian and member of the track team, as president of the senior class. Alice and her Theodorics nominated me as their candidate for president. Paul and I were pitted against each other in college politics. The Theodorics were defeated badly. My girlfriend, Ruth, never mentioned her political victory and Axtell appointed me to head the commencement arrangements committee.

Although I didn't know it at the time, Ruth and I would soon go our separate ways. She graduated from K-State in 1928 and accepted a position as a dietitian in Minneapolis, Minnesota. I placed a law degree above matrimony. She did not wait for me to finish law school. While living in Minneapolis, Ruth met a businessman named George Robinson, whom she married. However, we remained friends for life.

My aunt Edna, like my mother, was both father and mother to her children. In the spring of 1927, she received her Masters Degree at the same time I received my Bachelor's. She was ready to start a new career, and I was ready for law school. She was offered a position on the faculty at the University of Nebraska in Lincoln. She changed my life forever when she invited me to become a part of her family, live with them in Lincoln, and attend law school. Before attending the University of Nebraska College of Law, I spent my summer cooking meals and selling aluminum utensils in Iowa. I learned much about cooking and dietetics, but I was a poor salesman.

8   "Flower in the Crannied Wall" by Alfred, Lord Tennyson, 1869.

9   Epworth League was a popular youth organization of the Methodist Episcopal Church. In 1884, a precursor to the organization, the Oxford League, was begun by Rev. John H. Vincent in Cleveland, Ohio. In May, 1889, a convention of five young people's Christian organizations led to the establishment of the Epworth League which, according to the Annual Report for 1892, was designed "to embrace all our young people, and to promote in them a spiritual, intelligent, loyal and working Christian character."

10 In those days, debate clubs were known as forensic clubs and the study of debate was the study of forensics. This can be confusing to today's readers who are familiar with forensic medicine. Webster's dictionary gives two distinct definitions of *forensic*: the first relates to debate, "belonging to, used in, or suitable to courts of judicature or to public discussion and debate." The second definition relates to medicine.

Lincoln, Nebraska

Lincoln, Nebraska in 1927 was a town of some 50,000 located on the banks of uninviting Salt Creek. It was platted on this then windswept, treeless plain partly because of the promise of a lucrative salt mine. The salt mine never materialized but the state capitol, a state university, and two church-connected colleges did. Lincoln was a study in contradictions. Strongly conservative, its spokesman was the liberal leader in the U.S. Senate, George W. Norris. In 1920, it had junked the idea of all the other states that a state capitol in architectural design should be a miniature of the U.S. capitol. It came up with a radical revolutionary new design which would inspire architects from all over the world. Conservative Nebraska prohibited state-bonded indebtedness, so the capitol was built on a pay-as-you-go basis.

Also, out of the bastion of conservatism had emerged a man of oratorical fame who emerged from obscurity as a 36-year-old lawyer when he stampeded the Democratic National Convention of 1896 with an electrifying speech which included these words: "You shall not press down upon the brow of labor this crown of thorns. You shall not crucify mankind upon a cross of gold."[11] William Jennings Bryan, three times the Democratic candidate for President, was himself a contradiction. He was an ultra-conservative fundamentalist Christian in religion who led the liberal forces of the nation for economic justice.

In the early 1920's, the University of Nebraska at Lincoln had become known as a national football power, but it also produced an academic child prodigy named Roscoe Pound, who became the leader of American academic jurisprudence, Dean of the University of Nebraska Law School, and then Dean of the prestigious Law School at Harvard.

When I arrived in Lincoln in the fall of 1927, the city was getting ready to expand its population by annexing a suburb called University Place, the citadel of

Methodism and home of Nebraska Wesleyan University. My aunt had rented a large two-story house two blocks from the East Campus of the University of Nebraska, then known as the Ag Campus. It was located about a mile from the main campus of the university. This would be home for my first year in Lincoln.

The University of Nebraska College of Law was housed in an old brick building at the intersection of 10th and R Streets on the southwest corner of the downtown campus. In this building that held good teachers, good friends, and a reverence for the law, the kid from Wildcat Creek prepared himself for life in the courtrooms of America.

The roaring twenties were still in full bloom. I remember very clearly that President Wilson and our policy makers had promised the American people we were fighting World War I to end all war. Many young people had died in that war with a promise that this was their mission. In 1928, President Coolidge, in an attempt to carry out this commitment, sent Secretary of State Frank Billings Kellogg to an international meeting in Paris to draft a treaty outlawing war. This resulted in the Kellogg-Briand Pact between the major nations outlawing war between nations.[12] Coolidge no doubt erroneously felt that this treaty would be more effective in preserving peace than the earlier League of Nations treaty which our country refused to ratify. In 1928 fifteen nations led by France and the United States, ratified this the Kellogg-Briand Pact. These included Great Britain, Italy, Belgium, Poland, Germany, Czechoslovakia, and Japan. Later, forty-seven others ratified it. This treaty was to prove a monumental truth. No nation, including our own, will always abide by a treaty unless there is a mechanism to enforce it. The ink was hardly dry when signatory Japan began its military conquest of China, and Italy began its conquest of Ethiopia. Germany was laying the groundwork for what was to become the most bloody century in history.

The country was prosperous and all we had to think about was mastering our profession, getting rich, and having a good time. People trusted each other, million dollar contracts were entered into with a handshake, violent crime was all but unknown, and people normally did not lock their homes. "God's in his heaven /All's right with the world."[13] So we thought.

It was into this environment at Lincoln, Nebraska that a young man from Kansas, armed with a college degree in general science, some small business experience operating his backyard greenhouse, and ambition to become a trial lawyer, went to call on Henry Hubbard Foster, the Dean of the University of Nebraska College of Law.

Foster had studied at Harvard and was a disciple of Roscoe Pound. He was an impressive, short, cigar smoking man with a protruding mid-section. His penetrating eyes and shaggy eyebrows were but a part of the trappings of the greatest teacher I had ever encountered. The Anglo-American legal system was his religion. He had a contagious laugh which caused his belly to shake like a bowl of jelly. This was why all of his students endearingly referred to him as "Shimmy."

When I applied to him for admission, he informed me that the law was a jealous mistress and that no one could be a good student of the law and hold a job on the side. It was this statement that showed me great minds can be wrong. One of my classmates, Rupert Warren, held a full-time job at the *Lincoln Star* newspaper while setting a new record for high grades. Shimmy was so impressed, he shipped Warren off to Harvard on a scholarship.

The history of developing our system of law came alive in his classroom. I learned there that the foundation of our legal system was built in ancient England, but that we have disposed of much of the ceremony which was a part of that culture.

Shimmy dramatized the law of property. For instance, in ancient England, the King or Queen owned all of the land, but his or her subjects were permitted to occupy the land and transfer title. Livery of Seisen was an elaborate ceremony where the seller picked up a clod of dirt from his land and handed it to the buyer, symbolizing the transfer of land. When Shimmy reenacted this transfer of title to real estate, his students never forgot it.

I will be eternally grateful to Shimmy for showing reverence for our legal system, selecting me for a special course on future interests in his office, and appointing me as research assistant to President Hoover's Wickersham Commission on law enforcement.[14]

Prior to World War I, outlawing of the manufacture, transportation, and sale of whiskey, wine, and beer was left solely to the states. During the war, a shortage of food developed. Since all alcoholic beverages are derived from food - wine from grapes, beer and whiskey from grains - a food bill was passed in 1917 which prohibited the manufacture of distilled liquor, beer, and wine. Congress then passed and submitted to the states for ratification the 18th Amendment to the Constitution of the United States which prohibited the manufacture, transportation, sale, import or export of intoxicating liquors. These were known as the Prohibition Days. The 18th Amendment became effective June 16, 1920. To help enforce it, Congress passed what became known as the Volstead Act.

As a result of this legislation, a new underground industry was created. Mobs, gangsters, and illegal liquor traffic spread all over America. We faced a law enforcement crisis. This was the condition which caused President Hoover to address the whole problem of law observance and enforcement.

Canada did not have prohibition so there developed not only wholesale visitations to Montreal and other Canadian cities for consumption of alcoholic beverages, but also international trafficking. My research job was to examine and read appellate court decisions with reference to alleged errors in law enforcement and procedures as disclosed in briefs in criminal cases.

Law school students were different than any students I had known in my undergraduate days. They liked to insult the Dean's reverence for the law playfully. When the Dean entered the classroom in the morning for a teaching session, the class would burst forth in song: "Shimmy and his lawyers were feeling mighty dry, so they all went up to Montreal to buy a keg of rye. When the keg was opened, Shimmy Boy began to sing: 'To hell with Mr. Volstead, God save the King.'" Instead of admonishment, the Dean first shook with laughter; then reverence for the law began.

I had some other great teachers who inspired me. Professor Robbins was an old man with flowing white hair and a shoestring necktie. Unlike his Harvard colleagues on the faculty, he was from Northwestern University. When asked what he considered to be the greatest law school, he replied that he did not know, but one thing he did know, it was none of those that claimed to be. He had a few years as a practicing lawyer and could be quite cynical. His specialty was pleading. We learned that actions in court are commenced when the party claiming to be aggrieved files a paper in court known as a petition or complaint. This sets forth alleged facts as to how the plaintiff has been harmed by the defendant. If the defendant contends that even if true, a legal cause of action has not been stated by the plaintiff, the defendant under the old laws could file a paper in the case known as a demurrer, which, according to Professor Robbins, simply meant "So what?" The court could sustain this and, thus, nullify the petition or complaint, or the court could overrule it and give the defendant time to further plead or answer the allegations. Robbins would remark, "The legislature abolished demurrers, only they didn't."

Other typical remarks from him were: "The chief cause of spontaneous combustion is a heavy mortgage rubbing against a thin equity." "One day, I appeared before the Supreme Court arguing a certain point of law when I informed the court it had decided the question one way in one case and the opposite way in another case. What is your guess on it today?"

Robbins loved to lecture on the evils of cigarettes and beer. He referred to Saline County as Saloon County. He loved Dodge automobiles and hated Chrysler. When Chrysler bought out Dodge, he felt betrayed. Though dignified and serious, he was expressionless when the class nicknamed him "Cocky" because of his cocky demeanor. Class members also wrote songs for him entitled "'Cocky' Wants Me for a Sunbeam."

Because of "Cocky's" serious businesslike personality, a classmate named

Ralph Slocum, later Lancaster County Judge for many years, thought he would inject some levity into a Robbins class. Nebraska, as well as other law schools, had adopted what was known as the case method of teaching. Both American and English laws were founded on what lawyers refer to as legal precedent. Courts of last resort would write an opinion discussing the case and applying the existing law in deciding the case. These opinions were recorded in official case books. Law schools would provide students with selected opinions which decided the points of law involved in the subject matter under discussion. These opinions set forth the name of the Judge writing the opinion. Students took their turn in standing to analyze the opinion and apply it to the facts under discussion.

One time Slocum drew a case with an opinion written by a judge named Folger, which he said reminded him of coffee. Slocum ad-libbed that coffee killed his father, who caught the saucer in his throat while drinking his coffee and then strangled to death. The professor put Slocum in his place by responding quickly that he was not surprised this could happen to Slocum's father. Then he proceeded with the case under discussion. I mention this only to show how ridiculous great people can be in their college years.

I was introduced to the subject of crime in my freshman year of law school. The course was taught by Sheldon Teft, a Rhodes Scholar, just a year out of Oxford University. Later he would become a distinguished professor at Chicago University.

The Kansas I knew and lived in from 1911 to 1927 was a different world than the one we live in today. Other than war, the one violent boy I knew in sixth grade, and a few kids' fistfights, the only violence I can remember reading about were one murder and one rape. I did not know there was such a thing as domestic violence and none of our relatives or friends had ever experienced such a thing as divorce. Crime was a world with which I had no personal contact. I lived in a community of law-abiding citizens who trusted each other. The Kansas I grew up in prohibited both the sale of alcoholic beverages and cigarettes.

Oddly, I made my best grades in this crime course. I have often thought about this course and how fortunate it was, in view of my work with the Wickersham Commission, my career as a county prosecuting attorney, chief law enforcing officer of the State as Governor, chairman of the Board of Pardons and Paroles, Public Defender in Douglas County and Co-Chair of Governor Nelson's Commission on Prison Overcrowding and Alternatives to Incarceration. In today's world of violent crime and insecurity, I am convinced we still have a long way to go in achieving security and justice.

One professor, Laurence Vold, a national authority on sales who wrote a textbook on the subject, was a descendent of Norwegian immigrants in North Dakota. He was so huge he found it difficult to find suits off the shelf that fit. His feet were so large they required special shoes. He had a mop of long hair hanging over his forehead that seemed to demand he push it aside frequently. He had a distinguished career which ended at the famous Hastings School of Law in San Francisco.

Out of this mixture of mirth and scholarship emerged a group of young men who were to become great advocates and dedicated public servants.

One of my closest friends and seat mates as a freshman was Archie Storms from Holdrege who made the highest grade average of any man elected to Phi Beta Kappa on the year of his graduation. He did not like oral argument and asked me to take his place on the Moot Court team which would argue before the Supreme Court of Nebraska.

There was Robert Hamer, about the sixth generation of lawyers in his family who was prepared by both tradition and temperament to be a lawyer.

Another of my closest friends was Bert Overcash, who would become president of the Nebraska Bar, public servant, and the best all-around lawyer I have ever known.

Other friends included Paul White, who would end his career as a longtime Chief Justice of the Nebraska Supreme Court; Harry Spencer, married and a year or two older, who would become a distinguished Justice of the Nebraska Supreme Court; Lee Rankin, who would become Solicitor General of the United States, Counsel for the City of New York, and Counsel for the famous Warren Commission;[15] and Joe Ginsburg, who became a leader of the Lincoln bar. I have mentioned others elsewhere in these memoirs.

My years in law school did not prepare me to try a lawsuit, but they did a great deal to educate me in the rationale behind the law, the history and theory about land ownership and the transfer of title, the development of the rules of evidence and pleading and why they were important, the rise of negotiable instruments, and criminal procedures. All of this laid an important foundation for business, citizenship, public office, and the practice of law.

The most memorable trip I took as a freshman law student was to Curtis, Nebraska. This was my first visit to southwest Nebraska, which was later to play such an important part in my life. My friends, Archie Storms, Joe Ginsburg, and I had been selected by H. Adelbert White as a team to judge a high school debate between the University of Nebraska School of Agriculture at Curtis and Cozad High School. On a cold winter day, I cranked up the old Model T, placed curtains on the side, and Storms, Ginsburg, and Morrison set out for Holdrege. There we picked up Storms' father's enclosed heated car and proceed to Curtis. C. K. Morse, the superintendent, would never forget that I cast the only vote for the University of Nebraska School of Agriculture in the debate.

When I left for Lincoln and law school, I had turned my greenhouse over to my mother. At the end of my freshman year in law school, I still had some unpaid debts and wanted to use my teacher's certificate to pay them off. I was offered the job as school superintendent and teacher of physics and history at Farwell, Nebraska. Since the law school year ended in June, and Farwell schools did not commence until September, I returned to Manhattan to spend the summer with my mother. With five years of college under my belt and a contract as a school superintendent starting in September, I obtained a job carrying concrete in a wheelbarrow on a paving gang west of Manhattan. The heat was near one hundred degrees, and it was a good workout.

After my construction job, I joined the Manhattan Little Theater and tried out for a play called "To Catch a Thief." The cast was mostly college students. I was awarded the part of the detective. During this play a near tragedy occurred. We were playing to a large audience. I was on the opposite side of a library table, standing, and interrogating a suspect who was sitting. The suspect was my friend, Fred Seaton. One of the props in the play was a pistol lying in the center of the library table. While interrogating Seaton, I absentmindedly started playing with the pistol. It was loaded with a blank cartridge which exploded a few feet from Seaton's face. Had this gone off in his face, it would have been the greatest tragedy of my life. It would have ruined both Seaton's life and mine.

Farwell was a small Polish town located about ten miles west of St. Paul. This was farm country. The economy depended upon agriculture. Businesses in town consisted of a grocery store, butcher shop, drug store, garage, pool hall, and a large furniture store that served the area. A majority of the students came from farms surrounding Farwell. Spiritual needs were met by a large Roman Catholic church. Even the few Czechs who drifted in were Catholic. Protestants were almost nonexistent. The cultural center was a large dance hall. Each Saturday night there was a public dance and people of all ages from birth to octogenarians came. Home brew was consumed like food.

Two rather historic events happened while I was teaching at Farwell. One was that in either 1928 or 1929 I received notice from American Telephone & Telegraph that they had discovered how to transmit pictures by telephone wire. They were exploring possible commercial and educational uses but the technology had not yet been made public. The other was that one night we drove to Grand Island to see the first talking movie which I had ever seen: Al Jolson in "Sonny

Boy." What a giant step forward in entertainment!

1928 was an election year. The Governor of New York, Al Smith, a Roman Catholic, was the Democratic nominee; Herbert Hoover, a Protestant, was the Republican nominee. Some of my students wore derby hats and came to school singing "Sidewalks of New York." I was a Republican at the time in a Democratic town and a Methodist in a Catholic town. I learned, for the first time in my life, the lesson of belonging to the minority in both politics and religion. It was a wonderful broadening experience.

I was twenty-three. My senior students were seventeen. The outstanding student in the senior class was a girl named Loretta Borzych, a second generation Polish girl of unusual personality. She loved to engage me in political controversy and caused me to question some of the infallible political and religious presumptions of my childhood. She later graduated from the University of Nebraska, married an Irish funeral director, and had two children. Shortly thereafter, her husband died and she took over his funeral business. Loretta was the first person of central European descent to become a friend for life.

I loved teaching. At Farwell, I taught physics and history, two of my favorite subjects. Dealing with the young human mind, inspiring, instructing, and motivating youth was something I relished. I saved enough money that year to pay off my debt and the law school was calling me back.

Few years in my life were more momentous than 1929. This was the year Nebraska compiled its statutes for the first time in many years. It was also the year one of the most earth-shaking events in our nation's history occurred - the Stock Market Crash on Wall Street. This was the beginning of the Great Depression. Banks were going broke, closing, and carrying with them the life savings of hard working people. Business executives, lawyers, and other professional people were joining widows and orphans in the soup lines. Homes and farms were being taken by foreclosure. The utopia I believed in when I entered law school came crashing down all around me. My grandparents' faith in the all pervasive wisdom of the Republican Party, the high protective tariff, and Wall Street financiers to know what was best was called into question. The political position of my high school student, Loretta Borzych of Farwell, proved to have more validity than that of her teacher. Anarchy was spreading through the farmbelt and our great nation was facing the most severe financial crisis of its history. I became convinced then that only the unused power of the federal government could save capitalism in America and our criminal justice system. I became a Democrat.

I was a junior in law school in 1929 serving as an assistant librarian there. I was a member of the International Debate Team, which pitted Nebraska against Oxford University from England on the subject of abolishing the jury system. I

Debaters of the University of Nebraska, and Oxford university of England, will argue the question of whether the jury system is necessary to justice, at St. Paul church, Twelfth and M streets, Thursday evening, Nov. 21. The debaters in the picture are:
Upper row, left to right—Oxford: B. J. M. McKenna, W. J. K. Diplock, and Richard Acland.
Lower row, left to right—Nebraska: Allan G. Williams, Evert Hunt, and Frank B. Morrison.

Representing the University of Nebraska in Debate with Oxford. (lower right) was also diagnosed with a duodenal ulcer.

In contrast, my senior year in law school was rather uneventful. My classmate, who was to become my lifelong friend, was a farmer from Colby, Kansas. His name was Roulier, first name, Penney, because his father was named Dolar Roulier. He managed the campaign which resulted in my election as class president. Penney became a prominent attorney in Kansas and a member of the Board of Regents at the University of Kansas, but he always rooted for Nebraska when they played Kansas in football.

I admired many of my classmates including Gale Davis, who became president of Mutual of Omaha's life insurance affiliate; Bud Merrold, distinguished Boston attorney; and many others who enriched my life.

Near the end of my senior year, I encountered on the campus C. K. Morse, the superintendent of the University of Nebraska School of Agriculture located at Curtis, Nebraska.[16] I met him when we judged the debate in Curtis. He told me he was looking for a history teacher and wondered if I could recommend one. When he mentioned the salary, I told him that I was the one he was looking for.

11 William Jennings Bryan, *Speech at the National Democratic Convention*, Chicago, Illinois, 1896.

12 The Kellogg-Briand Pact, also known as the Pact of Paris, was signed originally on August 27, 1928. The Pact's sponsors, U.S. Secretary of State Frank Billings Kellogg and French Foreign Minister Aristide Briand, had well established credentials in peace-keeping efforts. Briand won the Nobel Prize for Peace in 1926; Kellogg won the Nobel Prize for Peace in 1929.

13 Robert Browning, *Pippa Passes*, 1841.

14 George Woodward Wickersham was an American lawyer who served as Attorney General of the United States during the administration of William Howard Taft. He was known for his interest in constitutional reform in New York State and also for his interest in international arbitration as a substitute for violence and war. In 1929, President Herbert Hoover named Wickersham chairman of a new commission created by Congress, officially named the "Commission on Law Observance and Enforcement."

15 The Warren Commission was created Nov. 29, 1963 by President Lyndon B. Johnson to investigate, report its findings and give conclusions about the assassination of President John F. Kennedy. The Commission completed its task and made its final report September 24, 1964.

16 This school was named University of Nebraska School of Agriculture or UNSA.

Teaching at UNSA in Curtis

The corn was ripening on Nebraska farms. The grass on the ranches had turned brown and autumn was in the air when this brand new lawyer boarded a Burlington train for Curtis, Nebraska to teach instead of practice law. The curriculum was high school level for eight months and college level in the summer. Students were mostly from the sparsely settled farm and ranch country of western Nebraska who needed a residential school. This teacher of United States and world history was also asked to coach debate and teach an overflow algebra class.

I loved coaching debate. My four-member team debated schools all over Nebraska and Council Bluffs, Iowa. Team members were Leonard Krueger, a farm boy from Wallace; John Quinn, a ranch boy from Mullen; Ray Roach from Maywood, and Bill Hicks from Curtis. None of them had ever considered the merits of a great national issue nor had they ever been far from home. The subject was Governor Franklin Roosevelt's proposal for unemployment insurance. We debated both sides of the hot issue.

This experience trained Quinn to become a political leader in Nebraska. He became General Eisenhower's advance man in the south doing the logistics and making arrangements for the first Republican candidate for President to campaign in the south. Krueger had a distinguished career in journalism and became an editor of a Buffalo, New York newspaper. Both Roach and Hicks had successful careers - Roach with a corporation in Denver and Hicks as Manager and CEO of a finance company in Waterloo, Iowa.

I had intended to teach for one more year, but Superintendent C. K. Morse required me to enforce the anti-smoking and anti-dancing rules for students. If I discovered a student smoking on the street, I was required to punish him physically right there in public view. If the student was some distance away, I was supposed to set off on a dead run to catch the culprit. I refused to do either of these things.

One of my history students, Beulah Hall, was the daughter of Harry Hall, a prominent banker and contractor in Maywood, a town just six miles west of Curtis in Frontier County. She told me that her father thought a young lawyer could do well if he opened an office in Maywood.

I have always regarded teaching as the most important of all professions. It determines the quality of all of the others. Dealing with the young human mind, its inspiration, motivation, and development is to me the most important and sacred of all human missions. However, the thrill of matching wits in the courtroom, the search for justice in human relations, and the protection of basic rights of real people all became a factor in my professional decision. The thrill of advocacy probably prompted me to choose the courtroom and public office over teaching.

I left teaching and moved to Maywood.

A Frontier County Lawyer

Harry Hall was a middle-aged man of imposing stature. He could have played tackle on a Nebraska football team, but he never attended the University - or any university for that matter. I never knew for sure whether his constant supply of White Owl cigars was a personality prop or a nicotine addiction. He radiated self-confidence. His style was to give orders, not receive them. He was a Republican by heritage with no political ideology. He was president of the Farmers State Bank, the only bank in Maywood, which was rock solid even in the Depression.

When Hall decided to enter the road contracting business with a farmer south of town named Young, he bid on a road building project between McCook and North Platte, a highway that would pass through Maywood. The state asked him what equipment he had to perform the contract. He answered, "A wheelbarrow and a shovel, if the kid has not run off with the shovel since he left home." Hall got the contract and became a road builder.

Hall ruled the public policy of Frontier County with an iron hand. One of his political partners was G. C. Hueftly, master of public relations, banker, Justice of the Peace, investor, and advisor to the solid German community of Eustis, Nebraska. A third partner was Earl Watkins, a farmer who lived north of Stockville.

Hall furnished me with a free office on the second floor of an old bank building. Access was gained by means of a rickety old outdoor staircase. Then he selected a rooming house for me owned by Fred and Edith Faling. The Falings also owned and operated a town grocery store. Fred was a short, rotund alcoholic who was never known to work. He was a Democrat with a passion for political intrigue. Edith, known as Deed, was a tall, gangly, masculine woman, mother of two mammoth sons. One was a drinker and street brawler. The other would become the responsible postmaster of Maywood.

Stockville, one of the largest and principal towns of the county, started to wither when the high line of the Burlington Railroad bypassed it in favor of Eustis, Moorefield, Curtis, and Maywood. Harry Hall and his two allies were determined that Curtis, the principal town in the county, would never get the county seat. So the county seat, after many heated elections, remained in Stockville, which had shrunk to some 180 people. There were no city utilities.

This was the environment in which history professor, Frank Brenner Morrison, started his law career in southwest Nebraska.

Maywood had no Justice of the Peace. At that time the Justice of the Peace was appointed by the Village Board. I recommended a retired school superintendent for the post and also recommended a constable to enforce his orders. We needed a local court for small claims.

I started filing suit immediately in justice court to recover defaulted debts. We were badly in need of liberalized credit to cure this situation.

When New York Governor Franklin Roosevelt was elected President in 1932, we were rescued from this crisis. Upon taking office, he told the country's citizens who were suffering the effects of the Depression that they had nothing to fear but fear itself. Then he started a gigantic program of public works, bank reform, expanded credit, rural electrification, soil and water conservation, and a host of other programs known as the New Deal.

One of the first acts of the New Deal was the creation of the Home Owners Loan Act to stop home foreclosures by refinancing the debt through this government agency. I was appointed local attorney to handle all of the legal work connected with this refinancing. Many farm loans from the Federal Land Bank and other lending agencies became delinquent. Congress, under the New Deal, declared a moratorium and liberalized credit. Much legal work resulted from this situation. Gangs were taking the law into their own hands to stop foreclosure suits. I came to the conclusion that if the federal government had not come to the rescue under the New Deal, this nation would have had a bloody revolution.

Banks were going broke wholesale, carrying with them the life savings of their depositors who were often left penniless. Thousands were losing their homes and farms, millions lost their jobs. People were standing in public soup lines by the thousands to avoid starvation. I came to believe that the very existence of our form of government was at stake.

I was far too much of a humanitarian to see hard-working people without jobs, people losing their homes, skilled people standing in soup lines, all in a nation that had so much work to do. I called into question the political philosophy of my youth. The problem was so great that only the federal government had the power to solve it. I became a Roosevelt Democrat and supporter of the New

A year out of law school, Maywood, Nebraska, 1933.

Deal. I believed the government should support the price of farm products, liberalize credit, create public works, insure employment and bank deposits, bring electricity to the rural areas, check water and soil erosion, and regulate irresponsible gambling on Wall Street.

Believing in capitalism, I knew that the free market was doomed without a certain amount of government to control irresponsibility and human greed. I believed that the regulation of the flow of credit by the federal government was necessary for the success of capitalism in meeting human needs, and I felt that the New Deal and the Roosevelt Democrats offered the best remedy for social justice. The Republicanism of my youth had failed me and I became a Democrat, although I knew then and now that no political party is perfect or always reflects my thinking.

1934 was the year to elect county officers. All county officers in Nebraska are elected on a partisan basis countywide. I wanted to be county attorney for these reasons: 1. It afforded a free office. 2. It gave a young attorney invaluable experience, both in and out of the courtroom. 3. It increased acquaintanceship and potential clients. 4. It was a part-time job which paid a salary of $1,000 per year. 5. In addition to being the prosecutor of crime, I would handle all of the legal work for the county commissioners and county officers. This would give me a great deal of experience in budget, public contracts, and responsibilities of county officers, which would be invaluable as a part of my legal education.

I was the lone Democrat; the other three lawyers in the county were all Republicans. The incumbent was a prominent able lawyer from Curtis, Fred Schroeder. He did not file. Kenneth Williams, who had little income, little experience, a family, and a pile of debts was the Republican nominee. He sold me his library and said he would withdraw from the race, but he did not. I bought a second-hand car and tried to campaign personally at every farmhouse in the county. This was my first campaign for public office and, unlike my later campaigns for state and national office, was motivated solely for professional and economic reasons.

In January, 1935, Frank Brenner Morrison was sworn in to his first elective office and moved to Stockville. Loyd Nicholson, a country school teacher and Republican, was elected county clerk. He appointed another school teacher, Joy Wymore, as his deputy. All of us were single. Nicholson proposed we rent a suite of rooms together in a large two-story house. It had no indoor plumbing and was heated with a coal stove in each room. The following spring, we rented a one-story house with a floor furnace and started to batch.

I received my early education as a trial lawyer on the second floor of Frontier County's old frame courthouse. On the other side of the table were some of the best lawyers in the state: Fred Schroeder from Curtis; Frank Butler, brother of Senator Hugh Butler, best trial lawyer in southwest Nebraska; his partner, Walt James, later reviser of the state statutes; former District Judge, E. B. Perry from Lincoln; and his partner, Robert Van Pelt, who grew up in Stockville. Few young lawyers could have had a more formidable array of adversaries. The District Judge was from McCook. He was the strictest adherent to the rules of evidence I have ever known and he had no leniency with young lawyers.

This two-story frame courthouse, in which many famous trials were held, had no running water, electricity, or central heat. A coal stove was located at the back of the courtroom. The outdoor privy was some one hundred feet behind this citadel of justice.

Water in the courtroom was supplied by a five gallon metal water pail accompanied by one tin cup. The pail was filled from a hand pump in the front yard. Both the pail and the cup were placed on a stand near the Judge's bench. The jury, attorneys, spectators, witnesses, and judge all drank from the same cup. I remember when future Senator Carl Curtis appeared in the court as a lawyer in 1938. He refused to drink from the cup. That is the only case of refusal I can remember, but I can think of no disease resulting from using the common cup.

My first criminal case to prosecute was a rape case. The alleged victim was both hearing and speech impaired. You can imagine my frustration on direct examination trying to elicit testimony describing her ordeal with the defendant. The jury could not agree, the court declared a mistrial, and I filed a *nolle* - a motion to dismiss the case - at the suggestion of the judge.

There followed all sorts of cases ranging from burglary, selling liquor to a minor, to homicide and murder. I was also the civil attorney to represent the county.

The dust storms and the drought of the 1930's in southwest Nebraska were a tragedy. Calves were killed to avoid starvation. Some years there was no hay, corn, or other feed. Cattle often survived on Russian thistles, sometimes known as tumbleweeds, which I mention in my childhood on the Colorado frontier. These thistles are full of prickly stickers, which, cut while still green, may be eaten by livestock. They are a desert plant which can survive with little water. Many days the dust in the afternoon would make it dark as midnight. The wind would drift the soil like snow piling up around fences and buildings. Many people left and went to the west coast.

1934 had been one of the driest, hottest years in the history of Nebraska. Corn sprouted and died in the furrow. Pasture grass died. Dust storms starting in the panhandles of Oklahoma and Texas swirled through western Kansas and Nebraska often clouding the sun. Crop failures were added to the Depression as a cross these westerners must bear. Many people escaped to Idaho, Oregon, and

California.

Hundreds of pieces of farmland and almost all vacant city lots had delinquent taxes. The county board hired a secretary for me and asked me to set up shop foreclosing delinquent taxes. These taxes were not on improved property. Hundreds of abandoned lots and pasture lands were deserted. I never had to put people out of their homes.

In this little Depression-ravaged, drought ridden, dust choked, primitive town, I met people who would be friends for life: my sweetheart and mother of my children, Maxine; Bob Crosby, a young lawyer from North Platte; and Carl Curtis, a young lawyer from Minden. Carl had served as County Attorney on the Democratic ticket but joined the Republicans because he did not like Roosevelt's New Deal. He was to serve longer in Congress than anyone in Nebraska history.

Benjamin Franklin Butler, commonly known as Frank Butler, was then southwest Nebraska's most prominent and respected trial lawyer. Frank, in spite of his constantly present cigar, had a personality that immediately commanded respect. Hard working and loyal to his clients, Frank was a legal scholar who had studied under Dean Roscoe Pound at the University of Nebraska's College of Law. In 1942 he became my mentor and law partner. Frank's wife, Maundlee, was a tall red headed talented musician who frequently played the piano for my wife's solos.

Frank hated the spotlight, but he dominated the thinking of his hometown of Cambridge. He and his brother, Hugh, were very close. Both were skeptical of big government and loved the unfettered competition of the marketplace. Both of these conservative Republicans, however, wanted big government in the area of rural electrification, flood control, and irrigation.

While managing Crete Mills in Curtis, Hugh Butler was largely responsible for locating the University of Nebraska School of Agriculture there. As a U. S. Senator and Republican Party leader in Nebraska for a generation, he dominated the state's political life for years.

After leaving Curtis, Hugh became Nebraska's number one grain dealer with headquarters in Omaha. Hugh's partner in the grain business was Roy Welch, who was the real promoter of ethanol as a supplement for gasoline, thus creating a vast new market for corn.

Historically, farmers had been victimized by lack of credit and storage facilities for their grain. Both credit and storage facilities were expanded under the New Deal, as well as a vast new program of production controls and price supports. The program was known as AAA, the Agriculture Adjustment Administration. Stockville became the office for Frontier County.

This brought a number of new employees to town consisting of officers, clerks, and file keepers. One, the stepson of a farmer in the hills south of

Stockville, became Chief Clerk. Manford O. Lee was known as "Whitey" because of a generous crop of beautiful white hair. Whitey's only formal education was obtained in a country school southwest of Stockville known as Havana. He had been off the farm long enough to take flying lessons in Lincoln.

I became acquainted with this thin, tall, young man who strode the streets of Stockville with well shined shoes, steely blue eyes, and a determined look in his eyes. His rural background and lack of formal education in no way limited his self-confidence. He was cut from a different piece of cloth than his peers. He thought he knew more about AAA than anyone in Nebraska and told the officials that they were doing wrong. Whitey introduced me to his girlfriend and future wife, Rosalie Hakel. She was a farm girl with ambition to send her future husband to the top. She started by teaching him perfect English, grammar, and immaculate dress. Whitey had grown up on a farm where his mother was a slave to the washboard, broom, mop, the kitchen coal-fired stove, dirty dishes, no air conditioning or refrigeration, and an outdoor privy. Whitey decided the government should do something about it.

The de facto slavery of his mother and other farm women of the time inspired Whitey Lee to become a missionary for rural electrification. I shared his enthusiasm to emancipate rural women from these hardships. We formed the first Rural Electrification Administration[17] project in the area.

Whitey Lee, a bundle of human energy, was then given a job as manager of a project in Steamboat Springs, Colorado. One of his customers, named Barbee, was CEO of Vanity Fair - not the magazine of the same name, but the nation's leading maker of women's lingerie. Barbee owned a cattle ranch in the mountains. He was so impressed with this white-haired bombshell that he took him back to Reading, Pennsylvania where Whitey climbed the corporate ladder to become CEO, build a vast clothing conglomerate, and have great impact on the way we do business. Among the things he instituted were the factory outlets so common today. What a classic example of what human energy can do even for a kid from the isolated country of southwest Nebraska.

Medicine Creek was an important tributary that visited Maywood, Curtis, and Stockville on its way to join the Republican River at Cambridge. Originally, it was a meandering little stream winding its way through the narrow valley carved by prehistoric waters. Man's greed for more fertile bottomland caused him to straighten the channel. Mother Nature decided to show man who was boss. Around Memorial Day, 1935, a storm developed on the Upper Republican Watershed, the like of which the white man had never seen. Unheard of quantities of water were dumped in a few hours. Walls of water came rolling down Medicine Creek destroying every bridge in its path and converting the streambed into a channel wide enough to do justice to a larger river. People were drowned and millions of dollars of good bottomland were destroyed. The raging waters of the Republican entered the Kansas River at Junction City, Kansas putting downtown Manhattan, North Topeka, and a part of Kansas City under water. Frontier County did not begin to have the resources to rebuild the bridges on Medicine Creek. After the flood was over, the drought and dust storms continued for the remainder of the decade with gradually abating intensity.

Shortly after Nicholson, Wymore, and I set up housekeeping, I accompanied Nicholson to the ranch home of Joe and Leona Luther on Medicine Creek below Stockville. I saw on the piano a picture of a girl high school graduate I could not erase from my mind. Nicholson informed me that it was his former landlady's younger sister. In July, 1935, while we were still wrestling with the ravages of the flood, Maxine Elizabeth Hepp, a young rural school teacher from Greeley, Nebraska came to visit her sister. At the time I had been dating a neighbor girl. Nicholson got a date with Maxine and invited me and my date to go with them to the Fourth of July Rodeo in North Platte. Wymore had seen Miss Hepp and was so enchanted that he decided not to get a date but go along to entertain Maxine. Maxine appeared in our front yard with my two roommates. I took one look and have never been the same since.

Upon arrival in North Platte, we went to the carnival grounds where we encountered a Gypsy fortune-teller who, for a fee, wanted to tell Maxine's fortune. The curious males could not resist paying the fee. She examined Maxine's hand and told the most incredible story. She said she was going to marry a dark haired professional man, have three children, two boys and a girl, never be rich, but always have enough.

After the hot, dusty afternoon, we rented a hotel room so the girls could freshen up. Then we went to the big dance at Jeffers Pavillion. While dancing with Maxine, I asked her for a date. From then on, it was intense romance. Within a few weeks, we were engaged to marry the following June. That fall, we drove to Omaha to pick out her diamond. She wore this during her final year of teaching country school near Greeley. This beautiful young woman with an engaging personality had a singing voice like I had never heard off the professional stage.

The winter of 1935-36 was the most severe a white man had ever known in Nebraska. My frequent trips to Greeley to meet Maxine at her snowbound boarding house are the stuff no novelist would believe. I made arrangements for my two roommates to move out and I remodeled the house with indoor plumbing, anticipating the arrival of my new bride. The plumber's young son was amazed at the installation of the bathtub. He had never before heard of anyone sitting in his dirty bath water.

60

Maxine Elizabeth Hepp, high school graduation

On June 28, 1936, our wedding was held at St. Paul's Methodist Church in Lincoln, Nebraska. My wife's home was in Greeley, Nebraska, but that location was not easily accessible to our guests. My Aunt Flora Edna Snyder, who lived in Lincoln, was almost like a mother to me. My wife's favorite aunt also lived in Lincoln. My Aunt Edna wanted to hold a reception for us and my mother, who was still working, found it much easier to come to Lincoln. Maxine's mother also found it relatively easy to travel to Lincoln where she could stay with her relative. In addition, St. Paul's Methodist Church in Lincoln held some sentimental value because this was the church in which I represented the University of Nebraska in a historic debate with Oxford University of England on the subject of abolishing the jury system.

After the reception, we motored to Omaha's Paxton Hotel for our honeymoon. We spent the next day with Lawrence Youngman, *World-Herald* reporter and my friend from K-State. Youngman took the story of our wedding to his newspaper but it was rejected because my wife and I were not sufficiently prominent.

After this insult, we left for Des Moines to visit friends of Maxine. We also went to Chicago to spend time with my law school friend, Carl Marold and his wife. From there, it was on to Niagara Falls, New York City, Washington, D.C., and back to Stockville.

17 By the early 1930's, although about 90 percent of urban dwellers had electricity in their homes, only ten percent of farmers did. Nebraska's Senator from McCook, George Norris, was a persistent advocate of rural electrification. It took many years of wrangling with Congress and the Senate to accomplish this, but in 1935, President Franklin D. Roosevelt created the Rural Electrification Administration by Executive Order. The impact and significance of the REA cannot be overestimated.

Life in Stockville

As I started married life in Stockville in 1936, this part of the Great Plains was experiencing the worst drought in its history. Dust storms blackened the sky. Many farms were abandoned and human endurance was badly tested. The heat in the unairconditioned homes was all but unbearable. I wanted to build a family and a career so I gritted my teeth and endured it. In Stockville I earned my spurs as a trial lawyer.

Frontier County was part of the 14th Judicial District which consisted of Gosper and Furnas Counties on the east and extended west to the Colorado line taking in Frontier, Red Willow, Hayes, Hitchcock, Perkins, Chase, and Dundy. Good lawyers like Frank Butler rode the circuit. The only District Judge, Charles Eldred, held jury sessions and equity or motion hearings in all of the counties.

It was amazing that either our son, Biff, a future Montana Supreme Court Judge, or I ever survived our life in Stockville. Biff's brush with death occurred when he was about two years old. We had installed electricity in our home, referred to as the Crawford House. Maxine had a tank-type vacuum cleaner. It was connected to the power source by a cord, one end of which was connected to a wall plug and the other to the tank. The copper connecting prongs at the tank end of the cord were covered by a substance called Bakolite which was partially cracked away exposing the electrified prongs.

Biff was a curious child. When his mother stopped the cleaner by disconnecting the cord from the tank, Biff, on all fours, put the plug in his mouth and was electrocuted. His stunned mother, instead of disconnecting the cord at the wall, pulled the live plug from his mouth. This was a traumatic injury.

I had been in Hayes Center for business. When I returned that evening, Biff's face had swollen to the point where it resembled a pig's face, but we were thankful he was still living.

Several Sundays later, I was staying with Biff while his mother was singing in the Curtis church choir. Suddenly, Biff let out a scream. I tore into his room to find blood pouring from his mouth. I discovered a small artery was severed and pulsing at a good rate. I pressed my thumb over the artery and tore to the neighbor's with my son under my arm. Then I put the screaming child on the floor while I held my thumb on the artery. The neighbor and his wife called both the local druggist and the doctor from Curtis. Biff recovered nicely with only a scar on his lip.

My first brush with death came when Attorney Frank Butler called from Federal Court in McCook. He needed certain records from the county court in Stockville and other records from the Justice of the Peace in Curtis. He asked me to bring the records and the two judges to McCook in an hour so they could testify. This trip involved getting the judge and records in Stockville, picking up the one-legged Justice of the Peace and his records in Curtis, going from there to Maywood, and finally south to McCook - a total distance of fifty miles.

My car would not start so I borrowed a friend's new Chevy coupe, a one-seater, and proceeded to obey orders. Norris Avenue in McCook was then Main Street but had no stop signs. Totally disregarding the speed limits, I tore south on Main Street. When I entered the intersection bounded on the west by Judge Eldred's home and on the east by a funeral parlor, I encountered a car coming from the west. We collided with such force that the car I was driving jumped ten feet in the air, landed on its back, jumped up again, landed on its rubber tires, and kept rolling until it landed across the street in the deputy sheriff's yard. It was a miracle no one was badly injured. The justice, superficially scratched, dirty, and bleeding, rushed to the courthouse and took the witness stand. My friend's car was a total wreck. Why we all survived, I will never know. When Frank Butler apologized for the appearance of his witness, E. B. Perry from Lincoln,[18] opposing counsel, wisecracked that was the way he liked to have his witness look.

My wife's sister, Leona Luther and her husband, Joe, had a nephew, Bob Luther, who was a star player on Nebraska's Rose Bowl bound football team. They were scheduled to play Stanford on January 1, 1941. So his parents, Walt and Zola Luther, Maxine, who was pregnant, and I, took our new Chevrolet and left for Pasadena. We left Biff and his baby brother, David Jon, in the care of Maxine's parents.

After the game, we went to the team dressing room where a player handed us a telegram that had been sent in care of Coach Biff Jones at the Rose Bowl. "Biff sick in hospital in McCook. Call Dr. Reed at once." Those words were branded

Frank and Maxine on their wedding day.

Our first home in Stockville.

on my brain. I was sure Biff was dead if they would send a telegram to the Rose Bowl. I grabbed Walt Luther, rushed to the nearest phone, and had him put through the call. Dr. Reed told us Biff had indigestion that was not life threatening but he thought we should start home. When I returned with the news to the team dressing room, my pregnant wife fainted. We were driven to the hotel with the team and a police escort.

Upon returning home we found Biff in good health playing with the sisters and nurses at St. Catherine's Hospital. I am eternally grateful that the shock did not cause Maxine a miscarriage. The incident was so traumatic to me that I think it was responsible for triggering a depression for which I sought medical help. Now when I think back on this traumatic news which we received in Pasadena at the Rose Bowl, it makes me shudder.

My wife was pregnant with our daughter Jean. Had she miscarried, our family, her family, the City of Denver and America would have lost one of the most inspiring people I have ever known. As a child, she attracted people like a magnet. She was a member of the student council and was chosen homecoming queen at Lincoln High School. She was selected by Don Clifton[19] for a project on developing positive human qualities. She graduated from the University of Nebraska. Later she became a Civic Leader in Denver, was Chairman of the Volunteers of America, and was an acknowledged authority on charitable giving. All this in addition to being wife of Denver's distinguished forensic pathologist and mother of two wonderful daughters. Jean has all those qualities needed in a world far too often dominated by greed, hate, revenge, and violence. What a tragedy if we had lost her.

When I started my practice in Frontier County, oral history of the old Frontier County was still alive. In the early days, court cases were the main source of entertainment.

Charley Tanner and Jim White were two old lawyers in Curtis who frequently tangled in court. Both were long dead when I had first arrived in Curtis as a teacher in 1931. I knew very little about them except that the stories about their activity still survived. It seems both of them were alcoholics who substituted theatrics for both facts and law. Rather than discuss the facts or the law they would wage a scurrilous attack on opposing counsel's character to prejudice the jury against his cause. The story goes that frequently after such an attack, the lawyers would meet behind the courthouse and drink whiskey together.

Frank Butler told the story about one of his first cases after law school. Knute Hall, a resident of Curtis, came to employ him to assist Jim White in a lawsuit. Frank told Knute he had no experience and asked why Knute would hire him to assist an experienced lawyer like Jim White. Hall's response was that he was hiring Jim White to try the case, but wanted to hire Butler to police Jim White. We were taught nothing of this nature in law school.

During my tenure in Frontier County, the main example of a lawyer who relied on oratory rather than the law and the facts to advance his client's cause was a farmer who had been admitted to the bar. He owned one suit of clothes, a loud green plaid which he reserved for court appearances. His oratory would have done credit to any modern television evangelist.

The human appetite for conflict, fantasy, and entertainment has always been a problem in highly publicized jury trials. The fact remains, however, that the jury system has become an integral part of the American brand of justice and democracy. Jury service is the only time in the lives of thousands of Americans that they actually participate in the important decision making process of government. Twelve people also have a tendency to override the individual prejudices of one person that can be so dangerous in the administration of justice. In our adversarial system, it is always the responsibility of the judge to hold the lawyers to the time-tested rules of evidence in our search for truth.

In all courts above the Justice of the Peace level, court proceedings are taken down in shorthand or by machine by a person called the court reporter, who is appointed by the judge and is a court official. These are then typed up and made part of the permanent record of the case. This record of what transpired is necessary if the case is appealed so that the appellate court can examine it for possible error in passing judgment on whether to reverse or affirm the case.

Judge Eldred's court reporter was a short man with a severe hunchback. Unlike the judge, he was sympathetic to young lawyers. When I attended law school, students were provided no experience trying either a real or mock case. At first, I had great difficulty laying the proper foundation for testimony involving conversations. The judge would sustain objections to testimony for want of foundation without any hint as to why. During recess, the reporter came to my rescue. He said the key consists of the four W's. They stand for: *Who* was present? *When* did it take place? *Where* did it take place? *What* was said? It was all so simple, yet I still see lawyers forgetting some of the W's. When I hear either lawyers or laymen criticize the court for exclusion of evidence on the grounds of irrelevance or lack of foundation, I like to remind them that there is a reason for all of these rules formulated over centuries of experience in our search for truth and justice.

1940 was an eventful year. The rains came back. The dustbowl became history. The New Deal had given us deposit insurance, a foreclosure moratorium, the Federal Farm Mortgage Corporation, lowered interest rates, rural electrification, soil and water conservation, and price supports for farm commodities, a host of alphabetical agencies, a vast system of public works was inaugurated, and the nation was on the way to recovery. Farmers were getting restless over acreage controls.

Resurgence of the Republican Party in Nebraska was impending. Carl Curtis became a Republican. The 1940 Republican landslide swept the statehouse, Congress, and the Senate.

1940 marked the beginning of my participation in state and national politics. Believing the New Deal philosophy was necessary for economic stability and social justice, I decided to remain a Democrat and was elected National Committeeman of the Young Democrats.

Jim Quigley, an aggressive, powerful figure of a man, a Valentine lawyer from the Sandhills, moved into control of the Democratic Party in Nebraska. However, Senator Burke and Governor Cochran, both Democrats, were not controlled by Quigley. When a breach developed, I accepted the job as Chairman of the Burke reelection campaign against Quigley's advice and he never quite forgave me.

The Republicans swept the state in 1940 while the Democrats remained in control at the national level. This put Quigley in control of all federal patronage in Nebraska, which he enjoyed fully. Control over appointment of federal district attorneys and federal judges gave the illusion of power, which was good for the Quigley law practice. This condition offered little incentive for the Democratic organization to elect high state and congressional candidates. I firmly believed that two evenly balanced political parties was our best chance of meaningful dialogue and good public policy. To resist this rush toward one-party control of Nebraska, I was to become a sacrificial lamb in a number of elections.

Even though I was a strong supporter of the New Deal, and felt that it saved this nation from revolution or collapse, I had opposed the President's court packing plan to enlarge the court, enabling him to appoint his own people and thus control the decisions. The Constitution of the United States does not state how many judges should constitute the Supreme Court. President Roosevelt became frustrated with the Court because some of his great programs enacted into law were declared unconstitutional by vote of a majority of the court. One example, the Agricultural Adjustment Act, was a law to rescue agriculture from the disaster of the Depression. It would subsidize farm prices by putting a floor under them through an equalization tax levied at the point of manufacture. Roosevelt asked Congress to enlarge the size of the Court so he could appoint liberal judges who would vote with the minority to legalize his programs. This became known as Roosevelt's Court Packing Plan.

This legislation was defeated in the Senate with the leadership of Senator Burton Wheeler of Montana and Senator Burke of Nebraska. I felt that, in the long run, an independent judiciary and a balance of power were essential to the survival of democracy. I was opposed to a third term for Roosevelt because I thought we were drifting to highly personalized government.

In 1940, I was elected an alternate to the Democratic National Convention. We occupied the same railroad coach car with the delegation from California on the trip to the convention in Chicago. A young delegate from Los Angeles introduced himself as the son of Senator Burton Wheeler of Montana. Senator Burton K. Wheeler, the fighting liberal senator from Butte, Montana, the copper capital of America, organized the United States Senate to defeat Roosevelt's Court Packing Plan. Wheeler announced his candidacy for the Democratic nomination for President. Unlike most liberals, he had opposed the Court Packing Plan.

When copper was discovered at Butte, the mining of copper and other metals dominated Montana's economy. Copper had many uses in industrialized America. It was the metal used in electric wiring due to its low resistence to the flow of electricity and, because of its ability to quickly transmit heat, it was used in cooking utensils. Great wealth was created in a few hands. The mine owners became known as Copper Kings and they dominated Montana politics for years. The Copper Kings controlled the courts, the legislature and the governor. Workers were imported from all over Europe and were exploited with low wages and unhealthy working conditions.

Senator Burton Wheeler became a strong advocate of organized labor, including John L. Lewis's United Mine Workers. He fought to give labor power to match the Copper Kings in collective bargaining during wage negotiations, and in negotiating for better working conditions. This was known as leveling the playing field. I told the young man I had always admired his father for being in the forefront of the fight for a level playing field for all Americans.

When I arrived at my hotel, there was a note in my box that Senator Wheeler would like to see me in his hotel suite. I picked up two members of our delegation - Bill Ritchie, a prominent corporate lawyer from Omaha, and Edgar McBride, a banker from Blue Hill - and asked them if they would like to join me with Senator Wheeler. Both agreed. This was the first time I had ever met a Presidential candidate.

We were escorted into Senator Wheeler's beautiful suite overlooking Lake Michigan. I had never seen a more impressive sight. The blue of the lake was almost unreal. Bill Ritchie opened the interview with this blast: "Senator, I am opposed to a third term for President Roosevelt. I am for Cordell Hull for President. I might be for you if it were not for your tie-up with John L. Lewis."

Ritchie was a corporate lawyer who detested John L. Lewis, the great shaggy-browed leader of the United Mine Workers. Lewis was an ardent New Dealer and supporter of the President's Court Packing Plan.

Wheeler was one of the most impressive men I have ever met. In slow and deliberate tones, he characterized Lewis as a man of the highest integrity and honesty. Wheeler said that he did not always agree with Lewis, but that Lewis did not demand uniformity of thought. He said Lewis would never lie and gave an example.

President Roosevelt, knowing of Wheeler's friendship with Lewis, sent Lewis over to convert Wheeler to the Court Packing Plan. Wheeler listened attentively and then replied, "John, someday a wave of hysteria will hit this country. When it hits, you and the people you represent will be the first to cling to the bootstraps of the Constitution for protection. You are now asking me to commit an act which will weaken the Constitution. I will not do it." Such disagreements never altered their friendship and respect for each other.

President Roosevelt was nominated and elected for the third term by a landslide. He took with him Henry Wallace as Vice President. Wallace was a liberal Republican from Iowa. He was a prominent publisher and a pioneer in developing hybrid corn. In reelecting Roosevelt to a third term, America did what it had never done before.

In December of 1941, Maxine, our baby daughter, Jean Marie, and I were in Omaha visiting her aunt and uncle, Hess and Leo Kunce when word came by way of radio that the Japanese had bombed the American fleet in Pearl Harbor. Our country was at war. The world would never be the same again.

Because I was building a law practice and had three young children and a wife, I had neglected to attend summer camps, do correspondence work, and complete other things necessary to renew my commission in the U.S. Infantry. Notwithstanding my family obligations, patriotic fervor led me to a physical examination at Fort Omaha as a prerequisite to granting me a new commission. It was claimed the x-ray detected a remnant of the old duodenal ulcer and I was rejected.

The Frontier County years were important to the Morrison family. We were living in Frontier County when Roosevelt's New Deal saved capitalism and democracy in America. We lived through the Bank Holiday, the Depression, the greatest drought in American history, and the dust storms. Many days mountainous clouds of dust would roll over the land bringing midnight in the middle of the day. Dust would invade the house and cover the furniture. It would pile up along the fence rows resembling the result of a black blizzard. Some years, no crops were harvested. One night, the air was so full of dust, I could not see the road or my headlights. Should I spend the night in the car or risk my life outside? I elected to abandon the car, feel my way along the borrow pit until I reached a farmer's mailbox, and then follow his driveway until I reached his house and rescue. By 1940, the rains had gradually returned and the dust bowl days were over.

I regard my years as county attorney in Frontier County as a valuable internship in the practice of law. As County Attorney, I was allowed private practice in addition to my work for the county which included being prosecuting attorney. Judge Eldred was probably the best trial judge in the state and I was opposed in court by some of the best trial lawyers in the state including Fred Schroeder of Curtis; Frank Butler of Cambridge; E. B. Perry and future Federal Judge Robert Van Pelt, both of Lincoln; and future U.S. Senator Carl Curtis of Minden.

Two interesting cases in which Frank Butler, E. B. Perry or both sat on the other side of the table follow.

C. M. Brown, the venerable President of the First National Bank of Cambridge, had an eccentric son named Clint who farmed in Frontier County north of Cambridge. He so distrusted banks that he kept his money under the mattress in his bedroom. This information spread.

One night, two masked robbers entered Clint's home and, at gunpoint, relieved him of his stored cash. After weeks of investigation, our sheriff was unable to find the robbers. Clint decided to enlist the services of the Cambridge town marshal in order to apprehend the villains. When the marshal arrested a suspect, I interrogated him and discovered he had not been near the scene of the crime that night. Clint and the marshal then rounded up another innocent suspect and arranged for him to go to work for Clint as a farm worker.

One day, I received a call from Clint informing me that he had shot his hired man. Immediately I drove to the scene and found Clint at the roadside, rifle in hand, with the lifeless form of the farm worker in front of him. Much to Clint's surprise, I told him to get a lawyer. Then I returned to the office and filed a complaint for first degree murder. Clint's estranged father, whom he hated, came to the rescue and hired both Frank Butler, the bank's attorney, and E. B. Perry to defend his son. The defendant was obviously guilty, but his resourceful lawyers came up with a unique plan to rescue their client from the electric chair or life in prison.

Counsel reported to the court that they doubted their client's sanity and ability to defend himself. They moved the court to do what had not been done before in Nebraska. They asked the court to appoint a commission of doctors, one to be nominated by me and the other by the defense. These two would pick a third to examine the defendant for his ability to stand trial. The court sustained the motion. The defense nominated Dr. James Willis and I nominated Dr. Roland Reed, both of McCook. These two nominated Dr. Nielsen, psychiatrist, head of the Mental Hospital in Hastings. Proving that psychiatry was still in its infancy, Dr. Nielsen came up with a theory that in his subconscious mind Clint thought he was killing his father and was of such mental state he could not defend himself. Clint was sentenced to the mental hospital and spent most of the rest of his life operating the store at the hospital.

Clint had been rescued from life in prison because his father was a wealthy banker. This is equality before the law. However, the bank triumphed over the mattress as a safe depository. The guilty parties and their loot were never found.

Another interesting case in which the crusty old Judge Perry was opposing counsel occurred in the ancient frame courthouse in Stockville. I had charged a prominent merchant in Eustis, Nebraska with burglary. The evidence showed that one of the defendant's competitors in the mercantile business was using chits to supplement money to promote his business. The defendant conceived the idea that if he could steal enough of the competitor's chits and give them to customers, they could bankrupt the competitor. The defendant had burglarized the competitor's store one night in search of chits.

Judge Perry, desperate for a defense, called two character witnesses. On cross examination, I asked the first whether he was dating the defendant's daughter and the second if the defendant had signed his bail bond. Perry looked across the table and asked, "What, no more daughters?" This was the ineffective defense.

Many examples of human error and of juries trying to achieve justice in violation of the law occurred in my early practice. In one case, my client had loaned money to her sister and brother-in-law to construct a built-in cupboard in their home. In doing so, they took a mortgage on the house. The loan defaulted and my client's sister and brother-in-law were forced to leave. Built-in cupboards are considered a part of the real estate, so they are covered by the mortgage. Before leaving, the borrowers tore out the cupboard and took it with them. I brought an action to recover the cupboard. The jury held that the cupboard belonged to the borrowers, but that they should pay damages to the lender for the wrongful taking thereof. This was an attempt to placate both parties although their verdict violated the law.

Another example occurred when transcripts of the case were not filed properly. In Justice of the Peace Court there is no court reporter. On appeal, the losing attorney must fill out a transcript showing the filings and the judgment. I recovered a damage judgment and the defendant appealed. In filing the judgment, the losing attorney failed to fill in the amount of the judgment from which he appealed. The District Judge, in reading the transcript, found that it showed that the Justice found in favor of the plaintiff in the sum of ___ dollars, court costs in the sum of ___ dollars, and attorneys fees in the sum of $5.00. This was so hilarious, the judge read the transcript aloud to a packed courtroom and threw the file through the air to the Clerk of the Court. He never ruled on the appeal.

I was doing well in the law practice in Stockville. We had purchased at estate sale a two story home for $750 and had landscaped it. Can you believe these prices? This home was near the top of the hill overlooking the town. We now had a happy home with three children.

I was in the last year of my second term as County Attorney when Frank Butler offered me the job of heading his branch office in McCook under the name of Butler James and Morrison. It was 1942 and my old adversary was to become my law partner.

18 E. B. Perry was a District Judge of this nine-county judicial district who resigned, moved to Lincoln, joined a law firm and then formed his own outstanding law firm in Lincoln known as Perry, Van Pelt and Marti. Though living in Lincoln, he continued to have an extensive practice in southwest Nebraska.

19 Don Clifton is an internationally recognized pioneer in testing human attitudes who now heads the Gallup Organization.

Life in McCook, Nebraska

In 1942, McCook, Nebraska was a city of between 7,000 and 8,000 population, the largest town in a territory embracing southwest Nebraska and northwest Kansas. It was a commercial, educational, medical, and cultural hub of the region.

McCook has long been a center of political activity in Nebraska. The only time in my life I saw President Franklin D. Roosevelt was in McCook. This lively town was the home of George W. Norris, one of the most influential figures in the history of American politics. It would also be the home of three future governors of Nebraska: Ralph Brooks, Frank Brenner Morrison, and E. Benjamin Nelson.

Since my arrival in Curtis in 1931, McCook had been my convention, seminar, medical, shopping, and entertainment center. This was natural since McCook is only 38 miles from Curtis. It was to McCook that I took Maxine on our first date. It was in McCook that all of our children were born.

The McCook courthouse was where I went for hearings on motions before the District Judge. Our annual meetings of the 14th Judicial District Bar Association were held in McCook. Living in McCook, I expanded my knowledge of effective advocacy in the courtroom.

This was also where my family and I learned the meaning of community service. I served on the Board of the Chamber of Commerce and promoted youth recreational activities. Maxine became a leader in community concerts. As President and then District Governor of Rotary, I had the opportunity to carry the message of community service statewide.

The statutes of the State of Nebraska had not been edited, consolidated, and organized in one set since 1929. My partner, Walter James, was a walking library with a photographic mind. He carried in his head the citation for every important case ever decided in the Nebraska Supreme Court. The crusty old curmudgeon of the Lincoln bar, E. B. Perry, was heard to have said jokingly that before knowing Walt James, he looked up the law and then manufactured facts to fit the law, but after meeting James, he discovered the facts and asked James to find the law to fit the facts. James was employed by the State to revise and annotate all of the statutory law of Nebraska which was to become known as the Nebraska Revised Statutes of 1943. This edition is still used.

James was the owner of a beautiful two-story oak woodwork home on the north edge of McCook. It had a windmill and an acre of ground. It was fully modern with city water piped in and a coal-stoked furnace providing central heat. When he moved to Lincoln, he rented the house to us. The following year we bought the house from him for a total price of $5,700. The present owners have remodeled it as one of McCook's more beautiful homes.

My growing income as a lawyer was supplemented by compiling abstracts of title in the name of Red Willow Abstract Company. In compiling abstracts of title, I noticed a man by the name of L. Suess had obtained oil leases on thousands of acres of land. Suess was owner of DeGroff's Department Store, southwest Nebraska's largest. This store had a feature I had not seen since my days in Manhattan. The purchased goods and the payment were placed in a basket and sent on a pulley overhead to the cashier on a balcony where it was wrapped and paid for or charged to the customer's account.

Louis Suess' first wife had died years ago leaving him with two daughters. He then married Ethel Oyster by whom he had a daughter, Eleanor. Eleanor was married to an Alabama farmer. L. Suess died in 1943. His present wife, Ethel, was unaware of a will. She petitioned the court for probate of an intestate estate. After this petition was filed, I received a call from a lawyer in Oregon City, Oregon who represented a daughter by Suess' first wife. The daughter possessed an old will naming her as executor. I showed up in court with the executor and the will. Eleanor appeared in court with her husband. The will was probated without objection.

This was my first meeting with Eleanor Suess Harris, a charming, talented musician, alumnus of Columbia University, and her husband, John Harris, an Alabama farmer and alumnus of Auburn University. Eleanor and John had two boys named John T. and Bill. I have never known a more congenial family. There was no ill feeling between the two Suess families. John Harris almost instantly became my client and closest friend in McCook. Eleanor became Maxine's closest friend. John T. Harris, while continuing his Alabama operation, moved his family to McCook, modernized DeGroff's store, expanded his farming operations to Nebraska, started a fertilizer business, and became a leader in McCook business and political life. Eleanor used her education and talent to lead cultural development, and establish the High Plains Museum. Eventually the Harris family

The Morrison family at the piano.

The ranch home that we built in McCook.

increased with the addition of four more boys.

The Harris family all but merged with our own. Maxine would stay with the boys while Eleanor went to the hospital to give birth to another. Our kids grew up together. In John Harris, I had a partner for civic progress.

McCook was emerging from the devastation of the great flood of 1935, the dust, the drought, and the Depression. The city needed many improvements. A city auditorium was built by the New Deal WPA program,[20] but the grounds had never been landscaped. The clay bank on which the auditorium sat was badly eroded. John Kelley, a pioneer businessman, had given the city a tract of land for a park that had never been developed. I conceived the idea of forming a non-profit corporation which we named the McCook Park and Playground Development Corporation. John Harris and I were officers. The corporation purchased an unused tract of land from the county, subdivided it into lots, called it the Circle Drive Addition, sold the lots, and used the profit to landscape the auditorium property, build picnic houses, and landscape Kelley Park. Steve Bolles, a retired relative of Eleanor's, volunteered his services. He rounded up donated trees and planted hundreds of them in Kelley Park without pay.

When the Army Air Force established a training base near McCook, the city was flooded with servicemen. We, along with hundreds of others, opened our homes to take in the relatives waiting to tell them good-bye. Friendships were formed that lasted a lifetime.

The government established a German prisoner of war camp and trucked the prisoners into McCook for work. World War II dominated the economic, cultural, and social life of the town.

My clients were forced to climb a long stairway to my office on the second floor of a brick building at the intersection of "C" and Norris Avenue. On the same floor were a doctor, dentist, realtor, and dental lab. When I officed in this building, the public was entertained each working day by Blind Sam, an accomplished fiddler who sat in front of the First National Bank directly across the street soliciting donations. In 1997, my son, Biff, bought the building, remodeled it, and named it the Morrison Building.

The need for summer activity for kids was met when Cy Young, manager of Barnett Lumber, organized a group, including myself, to create a midget baseball program including teams for both boys and girls from eight to fifteen. It was highly successful. The American Legion developed a summer baseball program for boys over fifteen. I have always thought these summer activities for kids were a factor in producing well-adjusted adults.

When I joined the Butler law firm, my secretary was a daughter of a widowed music teacher who gave private lessons in McCook. Doris Ann Stauder's education at that time consisted of one year at McCook Junior College. She was talented as well as handsome and striking in appearance. After two years, she asked to leave so she continue her education at the University of Nebraska in Lincoln. There she met a fellow student named Louis Lehr, the only child of a widowed mother in Elgin, Nebraska. They married. Then he joined the army to serve in World War II. When he was sent overseas, she came back to McCook and her old job in our office. After the war, Lehr came back to McCook to claim his wife. They moved to St. Paul, Minnesota where he climbed the corporate ladder in the Minnesota Mining and Manufacturing Company and converted it into the international corporate giant it is today. Lehr became a board member of the U.S. Chamber of Commerce, General Mills, Shell Oil, etc. The music teacher's daughter was socializing with the movers and shakers of America and the world.

My skill as a trial lawyer was enhanced when I met a young man from Oberlin, Kansas named Leland "Cush" Cushenberry. Cush was a disciple of San Francisco's Melvin Belli. He and I attended one of his seminars in Chicago. A strong component of Belli's technique consisted of expert witnesses and demonstrative evidence. Cush and I tried two cases in Kansas that set new records for plaintiffs' verdicts in both of these. One was a guest case; that means our young client, a guest in another person's car, had been rendered paraplegic as the result of riding with a negligent driver. The other case was a wrongful death.

These two cases were landmark from the standpoint that the Kansas Supreme Court had not affirmed a guest case for many years. The criteria laid down in former cases made recovery in a guest case all but impossible by making recovery dependent on almost intentional harm being inflicted on the plaintiff. In our case, the rule was relaxed and our judgment was unanimously affirmed by the court, thus making recovery in guest cases possible in Kansas.

In the wrongful death case we were confronted by the Kansas law which allowed a questionnaire to be submitted to the jury in the form of a special verdict setting forth a number of queries asking the jury to state the acts of negligence on which they based their verdict. If these were not consistent, the case would be reversed on appeal. The jury found the act of negligence to be excessive speed at the intersection of Highways 83 and 36. The act did not occur in the intersection but near it. We won the case on appeal because the dictionary definition of the word "at" means near and not "in." This was new law. The size of the verdict in one of these cases set a new record in Kansas. It was less than $100,000, which would be modest in today's courts but it set a new record in Kansas at the time.

I tried an interesting case in Hastings, Nebraska involving expert testimony. My client, McKeg, was manager of a chain store in McCook. He was involved in an automobile accident in Hastings which resulted in his being hospitalized in a coma for two weeks. When he returned to consciousness, he related weird experiences during his coma. In vivid detail, he told of his travels in the afterlife. He told of seeing human parts that were preserved and stored in barrels where decedents shopped around to pick out needed parts. This apparently extra-sensory experience completely destroyed McKeg's ability to manage his store.

My expert witness was a well-known psychiatrist and superintendent of the mental hospital in Hastings. He explained the nature of the psychological damage even though there was no external evidence of trauma. This was the first time recovery had been made in Hastings for psychological damage. The verdict, by today's standards, was low, but, at that time, it was the highest ever recovered in Hastings for personal injury. It was also the only case in which an award was made for psychological damage. I believe the verdict was around $19,000.

My adversary was a famous trial lawyer from Grand Island, Harold Prince. Prince was a pipe smoker who talked in a very loud voice. His idea of defense was to make numerous objections to questions in order to confuse the plaintiff and the court. Judge Munday, the presiding judge, seemed helpless to control counsel's conduct. He called many recesses in order for counsel to meet in his chambers and arrive at an agreement that would end the interruptions. After a number of such meetings, Prince refused to attend. The judge would then meet with me alone. This was unprecedented in Nebraska courts. During one recess, Prince went to the clerk's office and, in a loud voice, asked the clerk if the judge had ever taught Sunday school. He then advised her never to elect a judge who taught Sunday school. This was the only case I ever tried with Prince as my adversary.

My law practice had now expanded to northwest Kansas and southwest Nebraska. It involved the full gambit of human civil cases, but I had never defended a murder case. I was about to have a new experience. One day, I received a call from my friend, Dan Owens, County Attorney of Dundy County. He had a man in jail charged with first degree murder who wanted to see me. I asked Owens if the man was guilty. Owens replied that he was least guilty of the three that he had charged with murder and was the worst "son of a bitch in Dundy County." I reminded him that the man's reputation was not the charge.

For the first time, I took eight-year-old Biff with me to interview a prospective client in jail. We met the accused, Al Mathis. I admonished him that I would not represent him unless he told me the truth about what happened. He then told me that he was entertaining two of his friends at his home with a watermelon feed, the flavor of the watermelon being enhanced with frequent drinks of liquor. The party was in high gear when the victim attempted to crash the party to which he was not welcome. The victim then left to get a gun to force his entry into the party. Mathis supplied his guests with guns for self-defense. As the victim approached the party with gun in hand, all of them shot at his legs to prevent his advance. The victim fell to the ground writhing in pain when one of his guests took his gun, stood over the body, and killed him. Mathis had no intention of killing the intruder but had told a false story to the sheriff to protect his guest. I agreed to represent him. Local feeling was so intense it was impossible to get a fair trial, so I asked the judge for a change of venue. He also granted my motion for a separate trial from the other defendants.

Then I took Biff with me to confer with Leon Hines, a prominent attorney who had been appointed to represent one of the other defendants. After remaining quiet during all of the prior interview with my client and the subsequent conference with Hines, Biff spoke up and informed Hines that, "Our man says your man did it."

My main problem was the false statement my client had given the sheriff. At the trial, which was held in Trenton, I opened the defense by putting my client on the stand. Then I went to the back of the courtroom and asked him to talk loud enough so the jury and I could hear the truth about what had happened on the fatal day.

First, I asked if he believed in God. When he answered affirmatively, I asked if he believed he would be punished if he did not tell the jury the truth. He said "yes." Then I asked him to tell the jury exactly what happened on the day of the murder. He repeated the exact story he had told me in jail.

On cross-examination, Dan Owens asked Mathis to explain the difference between the story he gave the sheriff and the story he told the jury. Mathis refused, saying that he did not know he had to tell the truth if he were not under oath. The prosecution was stunned, and the jury returned a not guilty verdict.

One bizarre case taught me to never turn down a just cause simply because statutory law posed a problem. This case was referred to me by a lawyer in Waxahatchie, Texas. Another attorney in McCook had turned it down because the law was against him. The facts were these. In 1917, an itinerant farm worker came to the McCook area with a threshing crew. He stayed on because Frank Hoyt, a local farmer, offered him a job as a hired hand. This worker told Hoyt and anyone who inquired that he was a bachelor who had never been married. He had almost no living expenses so he saved his money and bought land.

Frank Hoyt was one of the few friends his former worker had. During the 1940's, Frank was elected to the Board of County Commissioners. The now well-to-do "bachelor" became ill. Frank took him to the hospital where the "bachelor" requested a lawyer to write a will. Frank called the county attorney, Charles McCarl. A will was drawn reciting that the testator had never been married, had no children, and was leaving his estate to his brothers and sisters, if living, and, if not, to their children. The addresses of these beneficiaries, of course, were not known. The testator proceeded to die. McCarl probated the will and Hoyt went out to find the beneficiaries.

Fate took Hoyt to Waxahatchie, Texas. There he discovered that the testator had a widow and children which he had abandoned without warning. He had completely passed out of their lives and they had no idea whatever happened to him.

The will was an obvious fraud on the court, but the law provided the will could not be contested after probate was completed. I informed the widow's counsel that I would see what I could do. Notwithstanding the law, I filed a pleading in the probate court asking the court to set aside the probate on the grounds it was fraud, unjust, and a travesty of justice. I kicked up so much dust that the case was settled between the parties without trial. Neither law nor equity had a remedy for a cause such as this.

One day an elderly man appeared in my office accompanied by one of his sons. He wished to retain me to represent him in preventing his daughter-in-law or her relatives from obtaining property owned by another son who had been killed by his wife under bizarre circumstances. He related the following facts.

The murdered son was married to Eva Hanthorne. The Hanthornes were a well-to-do prominent Frontier County farm family. Eva and her husband had no children. Eva was a devoted church worker and community leader. They lived on a large farm in Frontier County. Her husband had hired an itinerant farm hand from Arkansas. Eva became enchanted with the sexual prowess of the hired man who, gossip had reported, was also servicing some of the neighbor ladies.

Eva, with the apparent aid of the hired man, designed a plot to get rid of her husband. During the noon hour while the "Romeo" was in the field, Eva sent her husband to the basement with instructions to repair the water pump. While there, she doused him with kerosene and set him afire. She then ran upstairs, slammed the basement door shut, sprinkled kerosene on the house floor and set it afire.

The flaming husband escaped from the basement and the hired man arrived from the field. The house fire failed. The lovers panicked and decided to load the dying husband in the car and take a long road to the McCook hospital. The victim died en route. Convincing circumstantial evidence led to Eva's confession to murder.

Most of the real estate was held in joint tenancy with right of survivorship. The husband had a will leaving his property to the wife. The question was: Who was entitled to the victim's property? Under Nebraska law, a murderer cannot inherit under the victim's will, and there was no law or controlling authority as to joint property. Eva wanted the property to go to her nephews. The victim's father, my client, was the heir at law. Rather than to relive the horrible events in years of litigation, we settled the case by dividing the property between Eva's nephews and my client, the victim's father.

Before Judge Eldred was killed in a car crash, my last jury case before him was held in Stockville. I was living in McCook but my clients were a man and his family who were injured in a car accident in Frontier County.

One dark night, the family was going down a county road. A flood had washed out a bridge which the county had failed to barricade. The car plunged into the washout and my clients were injured. I sued the county. The road was numbered as a state road, but the state had not yet taken control and maintenance of this section.

I was confronted with my old adversaries, Fred Schroder and Judge E. B. Perry, on the other side of the table. I had the laboring oar because I was asking the taxpaying jurors to bring in a damage verdict which they would have to help pay.

Judge Perry, in his final argument, told the jury that it was the state's responsibility to maintain this road and not the county's. He also said that Morrison was a nice young inexperienced lawyer who was suing the wrong party.

It so happened that I had encountered the county maintenance crew working this same stretch of road the night before. In my final argument, I went outside the record to tell the jury that while the county was paying Judge Perry to convince the jury this was the state's responsibility, they were using the taxpayers money to maintain the road. Perry objected and screamed that I was going outside the record. Judge Eldred, at the time, was walking to the water bucket for a drink. He never ruled on Perry's objection, but replied that we had all gone outside the record. It was the first time in my life I ever heard a judge not rule on an objection. The jury gave me a verdict that they were going to help pay. This was a new experience.

The only time I ever saw a court proceeding degenerate into pure entertainment was in a trial before the county judge in Imperial, Nebraska. My opposing counsel was a lovable former baseball player, Bante Anderson, an alcoholic who showed up for trial half drunk. It was a hot summer day in the not airconditioned courthouse of Chase County. Anderson's client obviously was in the wrong so Anderson proceeded to approach the bench periodically, shake his finger in the judge's face, and object to the question. When overruled, he would say, "Appeal."

The judge had a number of pet squirrels in the yard which were tamed by the judge's constant feeding. They had chewed a hole in the screen in the lower right-hand corner of the judge's open west window. During the trial, one squirrel entered, ran over and jumped on the judge's desk. I still remember the alert eyes of the squirrel with his bushy tail hanging in front of this desk dedicated to the administration of justice. The squirrel soon tired of Anderson's threat to appeal. It jumped on the floor. Anderson promptly left his chair, went on his knees, and continued his argument addressing not the court but the squirrel. I have seen a number of "squirrely" decisions in my life, but this is the first time I ever observed a four-legged squirrel actually substitute for the judge, all with the acquiescence of the court and the helplessness of counsel.

On the 6th day of August, 1945, a new challenge was presented to human existence on this planet. I was taught as a physics student that the atom was the smallest particle of matter and was indivisible. I was later taught that if it could be divided, it would release enough energy to satisfy human needs forever.

Albert Einstein may have had the greatest scientific mind in human history. He was a Jew who escaped from the German purge and came to the United States. He knew that Hitler was on the verge of producing a new form of propulsion and that German scientists were doing research on splitting and fusing the atom. If they were successful, all of humanity would be at Hitler's mercy. Einstein sold President Roosevelt on the idea of putting together a secret group of scientists to split the atom as a defense measure against Hitler's threat.

On that fateful day in August, an American plane dropped an atomic bomb on the city of Hiroshima, Japan. For the first time in history, the basic power of the universe had been unleashed for human extinction. Seventy thousand people were killed or missing. Another seventy thousand were burned, crippled, or otherwise injured. An unknown number suffered severe injury or death from nuclear radiation.

I knew immediately that all of humanity was facing danger it had never faced before. President Truman had made the decision to drop the bomb. I was so unhappy with our commander in chief, I vowed to never vote for him again. I later broke that vow to vote for him in 1948. The Republican leadership was unanimous in support of Democrat Truman's decision, so it was no partisan issue. Truman, regardless of the fact that he was a product of the corrupt Pendergast political machine in Kansas City,[21] was one of the most sincere, honest, and dedicated men ever to hold the office. But I knew that from that moment on, no human being on this planet would be totally safe. The fact that the nation I loved would be the first to use this power for wholesale slaughter of innocent children and civilians was something I could not condone or forget.

Nagasaki followed Hiroshima and the war was over. We had demanded unconditional surrender, but better judgment told us to accept the Japanese request that the emperor be left on the throne. To depose him would incur a bitterness that could never be erased. General McArthur, a military genius who reportedly opposed dropping the bomb, was put in charge. Constitutional government was installed. The Japanese military was extinguished and the Japanese, relieved of the burden of supporting their suffocating military machine, proceeded to create an economic miracle.

I have many times thought to myself, why cannot all nations learn that it is far more moral and much cheaper to acquire resources through trade than through military might? McArthur proved in Japan that he was a master of real statesmanship.

After the war, four army buddies came to town and called on John Harris and me. There was no radio station in McCook, and they wanted to build one. I set about incorporating KBRL and the town was thrilled. All of this brought back memories from when I was an eleven-year-old. A boy across the street had some wires in the backyard from which he sent and received telegraph signals. This was during the advent of wireless communication. Several years later, we gathered in the Methodist church to hear a human message being broadcast from the college radio station several miles away. Radio was to become an essential part of modern life.

Eventually the KBRL boys discovered the station would not support all four of them. Three sold out to the fourth, Roy Lenwell, who stayed on, became President of the Nebraska Broadcasters and asked me to incorporate the new association.

While living in McCook, we found that our son David Jon had been promoted to the third grade, but still could not read. We now know that he was suffering from dyslexia, a condition unknown at that time. We took him out of public school and sent him to St. Patrick's Catholic School where he had much better teachers, but this condition plagued him the rest of his life.

On a trip from McCook to court in Beaver City, Nebraska, I encountered another brush with death. It was a bitter cold December day. The highway was covered with packed snow and the thermometer was 17 degrees below zero. Judge Eldred asked me to ride with him in his car which was driven by the court reporter. Beaver City is almost fifty miles from McCook. About two miles south of Arapahoe, the road makes a turn east encountering a steep, deep creek bank. The driver lost control of the car on the icy road descending into the creek valley. It went off the road and plunged head first into the creek. This hurled the judge into the rear view mirror inflicting a crushing fatal blow to his head. The driver's heavy fur coat probably saved her. Had seat belts been available in those days, the judge's life would have been saved. I was riding in the back seat, had ducked down before the crash, and had no external evidence of injury. I turned off the engine and told the driver to stay with the car while I went for help.

The car was standing on its nose and the doors were wedged shut. I knocked out the windshield with the bottom of my feet and started out for Lolman's home about two more miles down the road. When I returned, Frank Butler and other people had arrived. The judge's body was placed in an ambulance. The driver and I returned to McCook accompanied by Drs. Shank and James of McCook. Both the court reporter and I spent that afternoon in our home under the care of my wife, Maxine.

Several weeks after this tragedy, I was attending a bridge party at the Baumgartner home when all at once I developed a severe pain in the back of one of my eyes which gradually developed into a headache. Dr. Shank diagnosed it as flu and prescribed aspirin. My condition grew worse. I became bedfast and could neither eat nor stand. I called in Dr. Leinninger. He said the case was serious and over his head. He told me that only one person in the state was competent to handle my case: Dr. Jay Keegan of Omaha. I was placed in an ambulance, the sirens were screaming, and we made a mad dash for Clarkson Hospital in Omaha. Maxine and my secretary, Doris Ann, accompanied the ambulance. I met Dr. Keegan at the hospital at 9:00 that night. He asked about my symptoms and inquired if I had been in an accident. I replied yes, several weeks ago. This was the reason no McCook doctor suspected trauma. He put me on the table. A pressure gauge on my spine showed great pressure. He pulled out spinal fluid which was full of stale blue blood. My pain disappeared immediately with the pressure release. The diagnosis was subdural hemorrhage as a result of the accident.

I was hospitalized for surgery the next morning. The clot was spotted on the second trefine. A trefine is a hole bored in the skull. Washing through the trefine was tried for two weeks. It did not work. My skull was then lifted, the clot and sack were removed, and the dura sutured with silk thread. One side of the scalp was left intact to supply blood for the scalp during surgery. I was given a blood transfusion and two months later returned to my law practice in McCook.

My only full sister, who was so much a part of my life, met James Hunter, a door-to-door salesman from Westmoreland, Kansas. They had married during the thirties and lived with our mother in Manhattan while he finished college. He became an expert in breeding hybrid corn and moved to Waterloo, Nebraska with the Robinson Seed Company. He was an officer in the Army Reserve Corps. When America went to war in World War II, he became active and Hope followed him. They were parents of two wonderful children, Sarah and Bill. After the war, Jim bought an acreage outside Manhattan, Kansas. The children were ready for school in 1948 when Hope discovered Jim was unfaithful and supporting another woman. This resulted in the first divorce in the family. Bill and Sarah came to live with us in McCook and Hope went to live with cousin Charlotte DeArmond in Los Angeles where she obtained employment. It was a tragedy to have Hope separated from her children. We asked her to come to McCook where she bought a house in Circle Drive Addition. She became an LPN at the hospital only a block away from her home. Mother moved in to keep house and help with the children.

During the year that the kids lived with us, they became a part of our family. Both of them were educated in the McCook school system. Sarah enrolled at McCook Junior College, became a good secretary, and lived with us in Lincoln in 1958 where she was secretary to my Senatorial campaign. Bill lived with us for a time while in school at the University of Nebraska in Lincoln. After graduation he attended St. Paul Seminary in Kansas City, became a Methodist Missionary in Africa, returned to Nebraska, and is now a Methodist minister in Minden, Nebraska. Bill is helping fulfill the dream my Grandmother Brenner had for me. Both Sarah and Bill now have families of their own.

The war in Europe was nearing a close in 1944, an ailing President Franklin Roosevelt dumped Vice President Henry Wallace as his running mate, and selected Senator Harry Truman of Missouri. Roosevelt was elected easily to a fourth term. On April 12, 1945, Roosevelt died, and Vice President Harry Truman assumed the most awesome responsibility in human history. Shortly thereafter, Germany began the process of surrender. Hitler and his mistress committed suicide. May 8, 1945 was declared "Victory in Europe Day." The war in the Pacific continued. The Communist dictatorship in Russia, under Stalin, was a major factor in the defeat of Germany. Russia had suffered greatly in the German invasion and its occupation. Stalin demanded certain terms at the treaty negotiations which brought him and Truman at odds.

My life in McCook at that juncture was what most people can only dream of. My professional life was highly successful. I had a talented, charming, and loving wife, and three wonderful children. We lived in a beautiful home in a city with good cultural and educational facilities. What more could anyone hope for?

Still, I became restless. There was vacant land to the south of us and a block of virgin prairie across the street. My dentist, Dr. Dorwart, had his office on the same floor as mine. I asked him to become my partner in buying and platting the Morrison-Dorwart Addition to McCook. We sold the lots to our friends, reserving for ourselves those on which we intended to build our own homes. My wife and I had become infatuated with ranch-style homes. Dorwart built one on the south end of our acquisition. We built on the north end. In 1948 we moved across the street, putting our oldest son in the east ward instead of the west ward. It was there in the sixth grade that he contracted a romance with a small, lovely, talented child in pigtails and doll-like dresses, named Sharon McDonald. They became inseparable for life.

My life was so complete, I had no idea of running for public office. It was in this situation that I received a call from my friend Bill Ritchie, an Omaha lawyer who was then Chairman of the Democratic Central Committee. He asked if I would come to Omaha to chair and keynote the Democrats' State Convention. The Democrats had little support in Nebraska. Had I wanted a political career, I could have joined forces with my friends, the Butlers, in the Republican party and been assured of success, but I needed a challenge so I accepted Ritchie's invitation. The result was that the Democrats could not find anyone who would agree to run for Congress in our district, which was the south tier of counties extending from Colorado on the west to Missouri on the east. I was drafted as a Democratic candidate.

I thought firm price supports for farmers' crops were essential to economic stability. My friend and political rival, Carl Curtis, was opposed. This became the major issue in the campaign. Carl, with the aid of the farmers, won, as did the entire Republican state and congressional ticket.

The Democrats won nationally with Truman and his running mate, Senator Barkley from Kentucky. Truman's surprising victory put Attorney Jim Quigley, the Democratic National Committeeman from Valentine, firmly entrenched as dispenser of all federal patronage in Nebraska.

The run for Congress did not affect my law practice. My immediate thirst for public service was satisfied by being elected District Governor of Rotary the following year. As District Governor, I made friends from all over America and the world. The international conference that year was held in the Lake Placid Club nestled in the Anirondack Mountains of upstate New York. My roommate was a pudgy, ruddy-faced, storybook character from London. Japan had been admitted to Rotary for the first time since World War II. It was here that I met two of my closest friends for life: Attorney George Thornton of Kosciusko, Mississippi; and lumber magnate, Ollie Oberg from Sydney, Australia. Delegates came from all over the world. I was impressed with the potential of this service club to scale the walls of prejudice which separate the passengers on this little spaceship we call earth.

I never did lose my appetite for having input into the formulation of public policy. In 1952, Jim Quigley and his political cronies had decided to nominate the next president of the United States. Their candidate was the multi-millionaire oil man from Oklahoma, Senator Robert S. Kerr. Kerr was an able, dominating personality. There was no limit to his ambitions for bringing federal pork home to Oklahoma.

Tulsa, Oklahoma is a midwestern city on the non-navigable Arkansas River some hundreds of miles inland from the Gulf of Mexico. Making Tulsa a seaport would involve dredging hundreds of miles of the Arkansas River across Oklahoma and Arkansas and then going down the Mississippi River to New Orleans. Yet, Kerr succeeded in convincing Congress that Tulsa would make a fine seaport.

My independent nature and skepticism of political machines attracted me to a U.S. Senator, Estes Kefauver, who had upset the Crump Machine in Tennessee.[22] He was holding Senate hearings on organized crime. As a former prosecutor, this interested me. Kefauver had announced his candidacy for President. I made an appointment to meet him in Chicago. My friend, Orville Baldwin, a Tennessee native, was invited to go with me. I became chairman of the Kefauver for President campaign in the Nebraska primary which locked me in battle with the Democratic party hierarchy. The Nebraska primary was then only morally, not legally, binding on the delegates. Kefauver soundly defeated Kerr.

Quigley and I were both elected delegates to the national convention. Quigley refused to support Kefauver. Kefauver received, nationwide, far more delegates than any other candidates but not a majority. President Truman asked the convention to support the Governor of Illinois, Adlai Stephenson, whom I had never met. I felt morally bound to vote for Kefauver, the winner of the Nebraska primary, and did so to the end. Several ballots were taken. However, Stephenson received the nomination. His acceptance speech late one Chicago night was the most moving thing I had ever heard. I wanted to know this man who obviously was equipped to lead this nation.

My son, Biff, then fourteen years of age, attended the convention and found his own way around Chicago. He became a great Stephenson admirer.

I had enough delegates supporting me to succeed Quigley as National Committeeman. However, he organized the troops to support Bernie Boyle of Omaha for National Committeeman. The hatchet brigade was led by my old Creighton debate opponent, County Attorney Jim Fitzgerald. They cornered delegates in hotel rooms and convinced a large number of my delegates that I had offended Stephenson by sticking with Kefauver. This had not been Stephenson's position, but the false story swung enough of my votes to elect Boyle by a narrow margin.

Mitchell, Stephenson's Campaign Chairman, appointed me advisor to the Democratic National Committee. By this time, the political virus had infected this vigorously independent trial lawyer from McCook. The Republicans nominated war hero, Dwight Eisenhower from Kansas, brother of the young orator I had admired as a Kansas State student. Two able men of high personal integrity had been nominated. America and its former ally, the USSR, the world's two remaining superpowers, were locked in a cold war which was to dominate both domestic and foreign policy for many years.

Senator Kefauver of Tennessee would affect my life forever. He taught me how to approach strangers of all ages, introduce myself, state my mission, and move on. This was something I had never learned at any level of formal education. I have always marveled since then that we do not teach children the art of one-on-one communication. I also learned from this candidate for President never to limit your campaigning to the boss. When entering a place of business, a candidate should not only meet the boss, he should meet all the clerks, cooks, waitresses, and customers in a diplomatic way.

After we won the Nebraska primary, I was asked to go to South Dakota, aid in setting up the South Dakota organization, and supervise the circulation of petitions to get the Senator on the South Dakota ballot. South Dakota was solidly in the Kefauver camp and won with a landslide. The leaders of the delegation were the most prominent Democrats in the state. South Dakota was where I would meet the parents of the future longtime Governor and U.S. Senator from Nebraska, J. J. Exon.

The thrill of the Kefauver campaign gave me a new appetite for politics and public policy formulation. In 1954, I decided to run for Congress. The incumbent, Carl Curtis, filed for and was elected to the U.S. Senate. Estes Kefauver came to Nebraska to campaign for me. I picked him up in Lincoln with our Nash automobile. This car had a front seat which reclined and made a bed. Estes took a good rest with his always present eye shades pulled over his eyes.

After spending the night at our home in McCook, we took a whistle-stop tour on the Burlington Railroad from McCook to Lincoln stopping at all principal towns and speaking to people who assembled at the station. My opponent, Phil Weaver, was from Falls City at the extreme end of the district. After a vigorous campaign, I was defeated by this man who was almost unknown in western Nebraska. I even lost my hometown. This was a humiliating blow.

I had formed a friendship with a young lawyer in Lincoln, John R. Doyle, known as "Dugie." He had been a football player at Yale and held a law degree from Denver University. His father, Lum Doyle, was a prominent Lincoln lawyer and had been a football hero as one of Nebraska's famed Steihm Rollers. The Steihm Rollers were named after Jumbo Steihm, a legendary Nebraska football coach. The designation was a takeoff on the phrase "steam rollers." Dugie's grand-father had been a famous trial lawyer in both Greeley, Nebraska and Lincoln, Nebraska. Dugie and I formed a partnership, and in 1955 I merged my McCook and Lincoln practices.

20 The WPA (Work Projects Administration) was instituted by President Franklin D. Roosevelt in 1935. The purpose was to create jobs for people during the Depression. This important program used the talents of writers, artists, architects, and historians among others. People who most benefitted included women, children, African-Americans and other minorities. The program not only gave work to those who could find it nowhere else, it provided a sense of self-worth to those who were in dire need. Most of the literary and historical works produced during this time reside in the Library of Congress. Included are written and oral histories, records of theatrical performances, photographs, prints, posters, drawings, and other cultural artifacts.

21 Tom Pendergast (1872-1945) was the most powerful political boss in the Kansas City area. He was corrupt and controlling, a Democratic Party leader of whom the Party should have been ashamed. He was a bootlegger during Prohibition; he was responsible for underworld gambling; he bribed officials and coerced voting fraud.

   The irony is that he became a mentor to future President Harry S. Truman. Truman was an honest man who, at one point, risked censure by Pendergast because he was then a presiding judge who awarded a construction contract to a company not favored by Pendergast. However, there were times when Truman and Pendergast agreed on actions to benefit the community and, in 1934, the dishonest Pendergast sponsored the honest Truman in his bid for a U.S. Senate seat. Pendergast's political machine got Truman elected and Truman had to live for a long time with the reputation and perception that he won votes through dishonest dealings.

22 Ed "Boss" Crump was the undisputed corrupt leader of the Democratic Party in Tennessee during the 1940's. Congressman Estes Kefauver managed to defeat Crump's candidate in the 1948 Democratic Primary when Crump abandoned his previously hand-picked candidate, Sen. Tom Stewart, in favor of a different crony, Cookeville Judge John A. Mitchell. This split the Democratic Party. The rancor exhibited between Crump and Kefauver during the campaign and Kefauver's refusal to be tied to Crump in any way marked the end of Crump's hold on Democratic politics in Tennessee. Kefauver won a seat in Congress during the General Election.

Life in Lincoln

In the spring of 1955, my partnership with John "Dugie" Doyle, with offices on the 14th floor of the Sharp Building, became a reality with Norma Vermass and Dick Vestecka as associates. Maxine and I purchased a home at 17th and Calvert, sold our McCook home, and moved our family to Lincoln as soon as school was out. Frank Jr. enrolled at the University of Nebraska, David Jon entered Lincoln High and Jean took Irving Jr. High by storm. The next five years were to be some of the most eventful of my life. I commuted a great deal to McCook but gradually turned my McCook practice over to my partners Bill Lyons and Clyde Starrett. Frank Butler of Cambridge and I had dissolved our partnership several years before.

Before moving from McCook to Lincoln in 1955, my participation in politics had not prevented my becoming an experienced trial lawyer. I had, as previously noted, received what was then a record plaintiff's personal injury verdict in Hastings, plowing new ground by recovering for psychological damage. Also, as previously noted, I had obtained, with Leland "Cush" Cushenbery, two record verdicts in Oberlin, Kansas.

Upon moving to Lincoln, John "Dugie" Doyle and I had almost instant courtroom success. We reversed a former personal injury verdict against the Lincoln Traction Company with a defendant's verdict. Along with Gerry Whelan of Hastings,[23] we set a new record for wrongful death verdict in the District Court of Lancaster County. In this damage case for wrongful death, our client was a frail little middle-aged woman with several elementary age school children. There were two defendants. One was a farmer driving a pickup who entered the highway from a side road in front of an oncoming car being driven by the other defendant. The latter driver, in order to avoid collision with the pickup, swerved over into the left lane of traffic and hit our driver head on. This killed our driver who was a

Marine officer. The decedent's widow and children were entitled to monetary damage for the loss of their husband and father in an amount to be determined by the jury from either or both defendants whom the jury found to be negligent. The farmer had no insurance. The other driver did, so it was necessary to hold the second driver liable. Previous to this case standard, mortality tables were introduced in evidence to determine life expectancy and, thus, expected contributions to the family. In this case, we did what had never been done before in Lincoln. We called a professional actuary as an expert witness to testify as to the life expectancy of the deceased. We obtained the largest verdict which had ever been recovered up to that time in Lincoln for wrongful death. By today's standards it was very small, but it helped the widow educate the children.

From 1955 through 1960 this trial lawyer started a new political career. The Democratic party had sunk to a new low in 1956 when I decided to manage Frank Sorrell's hopeless campaign for governor. His running mate, a druggist named Long from Grand Island, died during the campaign and I consented to fill the vacancy as a candidate for lieutenant governor with no hope of winning. I did, however, finish ahead of the state ticket.

Don McGinley, a young lawyer from a prominent Nebraska ranch family at Ogallala, was elected Congressman from Nebraska's big Third District and Larry Brock, a farmer from Wakefield, was elected from Nebraska's First District. However, two years later, in 1960, they were swept under with the Republican landslide in Nebraska.

In 1957 State Senator Terry Carpenter called me from Scottsbluff and asked me to run for governor. He was out to defeat Governor Anderson and guaranteed to elect me. My only expense would be my filing fee. It would not be necessary for me to leave my law office or campaign. I told him that I was not interested in running for governor. At that time, my primary public interest was in national, not state, problems.

Terry Carpenter was a colorful Scottsbluff businessman who sometimes ran for office as a Democrat and sometimes as a Republican. He had little use for political parties. In 1932, he was elected to Congress as a Democrat from Nebraska's big third district. He did not run for re-election because he said that a taxi driver in Washington had more power than a congressman. He ran many times for the U. S. Senate and governor, but was never elected. I believe he remained a registered Republican until he ran for the U. S. Senate as a Democrat in 1970.

Carpenter built his own town between Scottsbluff and Gering, called it Terrytown and controlled its city council. Terry, a teetotaler, created a restaurant in Terrytown which served liquor by the drink at a time when Gering and Scottsbluff were both dry and prohibited the sale of liquor. He made a fortune.

In 1956, as a delegate to the Republican National Convention, Carpenter created a national sensation by nominating a fictional character named Joe Smith for Vice President. He decided then to become a power in Nebraska's non-partisan legislature and served there for many years.

He loved to give speeches live or on television. He was a powerful speaker with no regard for "party loyalty." As a legislator, he decided he was going to beat Governor Anderson by making speeches on television the last week before election so no one could answer him.

My wife, Maxine, approached Ralph Brooks, our school superintendent in McCook, and held a meeting at our home to promote his candidacy for governor. Bernard Boyle of Omaha pledged his support and Ralph Brooks became the uncontested Democratic nominee.

I succumbed to pressure from State Democratic Chairman Willard Townsend, the national COPE organization, and the support of the Kennedy family to make a run for the United States Senate. With few resources and little organization, I made a good showing.

Carpenter fulfilled his promise by buying much TV time on all three Omaha stations the weekend before the election. The ads made an all-out attack on Anderson and Carpenter managed to elect Brooks by a slim margin.

Brooks was not in good health, seemed out of place as governor, and had a burning desire to serve in the U. S. Senate. Robert Conrad, an able young lawyer from Genoa who had served as executive secretary of the state Democratic party, was Brooks' Administrative Assistant.[24] Brooks secretly decided to run for the Senate with Conrad running for governor at the next election in 1960. This was arranged with Bernard Boyle, the Democrat strongman, and the party leaders. My primary interest was still in national and international policy.

I had known C. A. Sorensen and admired him. C. A. was a liberal Republican Lincoln lawyer who became Senator George Norris' right hand man in Nebraska. He was active in drafting much of Nebraska's public power legislation. He served a term as Nebraska's Attorney General. He opposed the death penalty and said he wanted the symbol of his state to be the schoolhouse, not the electric chair. Sorensen was father to a group of brilliant kids, all of whom became Democrats. The oldest, Theodore, graduated number one in his class from the University of Nebraska Law School. Ted headed east and became a top advisor to Congressman John F. Kennedy. Ted became interested in helping to elect his boss president. As a Kefauver delegate to the 1952 and 1956 Democratic conventions, I had heard John (Jack) F. Kennedy give a speech. I was sold.

John Fitzgerald Kennedy, in 1958, was a young Senator from Massachusetts. Destiny had slated this talented, ambitious son of privilege to become President of the United States. He was one of the speakers that year at the annual Democratic Jefferson-Jackson Day dinner in Omaha. His wife, Jackie, was with him. This was their wedding anniversary and they had sacrificed their privacy for politics. After the dinner was over, he invited Maxine and me to accompany him and Jackie on their private plane, the Caroline, on a flight to Lincoln, Nebraska where, the next morning, he was to speak at a fund-raiser for me as a candidate for the United States Senate. That night, after landing, he gave me a substantial contribution for my campaign. The next morning after the breakfast, he returned to Washington, D.C. as a United States Senator from Massachusetts.

I came to love, admire, and respect Kennedy. I was impressed with his leadership qualities. My memory then went to the time when he called me and told me he had a room at the Cornhusker Hotel. I was in my office in Lincoln and he said he would like to see me. He met me at the door, just he and I alone, no secretaries, no guards - just two human beings, one on one, who discussed politics, public policy, foreign policy, our country, and its future.

The next time I met Senator Kennedy was probably a blur. We exchanged correspondence. He sent his chief aide, my friend, Ted Sorenson, to assist in setting up a campaign organization.

We set up a series of meetings throughout eastern Nebraska starting one night in Omaha. I had trouble bringing Bernie Boyle aboard because, being a Catholic, he did not think a Catholic could be elected President. No Catholic had ever been elected president. This was due to an irrational fear held by some members of the general populace that a Catholic would be subservient to the Pope in political decisions. Bernie, however, attended the meeting, was impressed with Sorensen's presentation, and the enthusiasm of the meeting.

The next day I was flying with Sorensen in a small plane for a meeting in Grand Island. It was on this occasion that Sorensen asked me to guess who called at his hotel room after the Omaha meeting. He then told me that Boyle pledged his support. I knew then that Boyle sensed the Kennedy bandwagon was starting to roll and he did not want to be left behind. This information was followed by Sorensen telling me that Kennedy would like a Scandinavian, Protestant farmer to be Chairman of his Nebraska Primary Campaign and asked what I thought of Hans Jensen of Aurora. I replied that if that was the criterion, you could not beat Jensen. Sorensen then requested me to ask Jensen. Jensen jumped at the offer like a hungry dog in a meat market. Jensen was now chair. Boyle, as national committeeman, became captain of the Kennedy ship in Nebraska, and Morrison became a candidate for delegate pledged to Kennedy.

Among the appearances I arranged for Kennedy was an appearance before the Lincoln Downtown Rotary Club. Never before had a future President spoken to the Lincoln Downtown Rotary Club.

Conference with President Kennedy.

This was the political environment in 1959 when I visited an office supply house in Lincoln that was operated by a friend from South Dakota, J. James Exon. I had worked with his parents who were leaders in the Democratic party in South Dakota, and J. J. had worked with me in the New Life movement in the Nebraska Democratic party. The New Life Movement was an effort centered in Lincoln to revitalize the Democratic Party as an effective instrument of government and policy making.

J.J. (Jim) surprised me by asking why I did not run for governor in 1960, knowing that Governor Brooks had his eye on the Senate. My reply was threefold: 1. I did not want to be governor. 2. The Democratic organization headed by Boyle was solidly behind Conrad, so my nomination would be impossible. 3. 1960 was a Presidential year so the entire ticket was going Republican in Nebraska and no Democrat could be elected governor.

Jim's reply was that he thought I had a chance and, at my age (55), if I was going to have any impact on public policy, I'd better jump aboard or my chance would be gone. He asked me to think before I said no. Several days later, I returned and informed him I would run if he would manage the campaign. He accepted quickly and began what President Kennedy described as the political miracle of 1960.

In the fall of 1959, Exon had me call a press conference while Brooks, Conrad, Boyle, and the political brass were at a meeting in Kansas City. I announced that Governor Brooks was going to run for the Senate and that I intended to file for governor. This hit the Kansas City delegation by surprise. When contacted by the press, Brooks was livid because I had announced his plans. Conrad was baffled and the Democratic party's news director informed the press that my announcement had "all the impact of a falling leaf."

Exon took over the Morrison Campaign for Governor in the face of the Conrad-Brooks alliance. He had buttons printed that read: "Brooks for Senate, Morrison for Governor." Brooks and Conrad looked helpless. There was one former Democratic Governor still living who had a run-in with Conrad when he was State Engineer. This was former Governor Cochran, who had retired from politics. Exon asked him to support Morrison.

Exon then persuaded another Democratic candidate, Charles Bates, to resign in my favor. Next, J. J. persuaded Conrad's nominal Pan Handle Campaign Manager to resign and announce his support for Morrison. In this way Exon defeated the formerly entrenched members of the Nebraska Democratic Party and Morrison was nominated. Brooks died during his campaign for the Senate, and the party nominated Conrad to fill the vacancy. Morrison and Conrad campaigned together in the general election. Senator John Cooper won a hotly contested Republican primary. During the general election, he made some mistakes which I capitalized on and the result was that Morrison was the only Democrat elected to a major office in Nebraska.

J. J. Exon was catapulted into the catbird seat of Nebraska politics. In January 1961, Frank Brenner Morrison, Sr. was sworn in as Governor of Nebraska facing a host of pressing state problems for which he must seek solutions without having any previous experience in state government. Morrison left all of his clients behind and his rising career as a trial lawyer in Lincoln, Nebraska was over. From now on the State of Nebraska was his client.

After election and before taking office as Governor, I discovered quickly that the governor is expected to know every community in the state; all the educational and economic problems; every road and highway with all of their needs; budgetary needs of dozens of state institutions; and how to solve the state crime problems, including who should or should not be paroled.

Before I was sworn in, Ray Smith of the Oil and Gas Commission, recommended that I attend the Interstate Oil and Gas Compact Convention in Phoenix. It was in late November. We chartered an airplane in Lodgepole, Nebraska. Our return was extremely dangerous. The weather was socked in, and our six-passenger small plane was forced to fly at 20,000 feet over the mountains, not only for clearance, but to keep the propellers from freezing over. Our coats were in the trunk and not available. Oxygen was so scarce, we barely survived. Such was my introduction to the hazards of the governorship. This experience was only a prelude to my airplane experiences.

On one winter day we were flying into Neligh, Nebraska. The snow was deep and had been plowed back in high drifts not much farther apart than the width of our plane. Upon landing, the pilot caught the tip of one wing in the snowbank and wrecked the plane. We escaped unharmed. A newsman who met us asked if I was scared. I replied not as much so as when I had a runaway team of horses.

The airplane made it possible for me to work a full day in the office and attend a meeting anywhere in the Panhandle that evening. One night we had flown to Imperial, near the Colorado line, for an evening meeting. We were fogged in and could not fly out. It was imperative that I be in Lincoln the next morning so we decided to drive to McCook and catch the train to Lincoln. The fog was so dense we arrived too late for the passenger train. This forced us to ride a freight train caboose into Lincoln. Fortunately, the mile-long freight train made only a few stops, but every time it did, riders in the caboose felt like they were being shot out of a cannon.

I would like to tell you about our family during our residence in Lincoln. Biff had entered the University of Nebraska College of Business Administration as a pre-law student. During his student years at the university, he continued his courtship with his McCook girlfriend, Sharon McDonald. She attended one year at McCook Junior College followed with three brilliant years at the University of Nebraska. She held scholarships; was Editor-in-Chief of the Cornhusker Yearbook; was a member and officer of the women's honor society, Mortar Board; and was graduated with honors. She and Biff were married in 1959. They moved to Denver where she taught in the Littleton School System and Biff entered Law School at Denver University.

Our daughter Jean graduated from Lincoln High School where she had been a cheerleader and member of the Student Council. She went to the University of Nebraska where she was a member of Gold's College Board,[25] participated in a special leadership development project, served as an attendant to the Homecoming Queen, and was a leader in campus social life. She graduated in 1963 and took a job teaching at Hinsdale, Illinois. While teaching in this Chicago suburb, she met a medical student at the University of Illinois Medical College in Chicago named Ben Galloway. They were married at the Governor's Mansion in May, 1965.

Our son, David Jon, graduated from Lincoln High School in 1958 where he was a member of the championship school swimming and track teams. After graduation, he took some work at the University of Nebraska, joined the U. S. Marine Corp and, upon receiving an honorable discharge, returned home. Then he met a lovely girl from Beaumont, Texas named Jerry Jones. They were married at Beaumont in 1962 where David Jon went to work with his father-in-law in the construction business in addition to selling life insurance.

During our residence in Lincoln both Biff and David Jon and their wives presented us with grandsons: John Martin to Biff, and Clayton Frank to David Jon.

23 Gerald "Gerry" T. Whelan was son of a Hastings, Nebraska lawyer. He later became active in politics and served as Lt. Governor of Nebraska from 1975-1979.

24 In later years, this designation has become "Chief of Staff."

25 Gold's was a large downtown department store.

The Inaugural Ball

Governor of Nebraska

On January 5, 1961, a 55-year-old man whose lifetime ambition was to sit in the United States Senate or the cabinet of a President helping to determine the foreign policy of the nation, found himself sitting as chief law officer of the State of Nebraska. His friend, Senator John F. Kennedy, was elected President. This created opportunities for cooperation at different levels of government. I knew that modern technology in transportation and communication had made the whole world a smaller community than any of the states I knew as a child. All of our major legal, economic, educational, and security problems at the local, state, national, and international level were interrelated. My job was to make the most of that interrelationship.

I soon discovered that the main problem of a governor, an administrator at any level, either in government, education, or the private sector was to discover the truth and to see that it was communicated to those responsible for its implementation without interruption or corruption. The discovery of truth, therefore, became the bedrock of all social progress. The capacity of the human mind for good or evil had no limits. Its quality was determined by the quality of what inspired it and the accuracy of that information. If we were to discover the ultimate truth, it would demand the full development of the potential of every human being. The search for truth as a basis for a better, more just, secure, and progressive society should begin in the home. Parents should be assured adequate employment, a secure and crime-free community, and quality education from preschool through postgraduate. There should be no form of discrimination based on race, gender, age, political or religious ideology, nationality or ethnic origin. Any discrimination would hinder the full development of any person.

Research based on a search for truth, rather than communication of preconceived prejudices, was essential. This responsibility involved making creative employment opportunities, a healthy and inspiring environment, and quality education with its twin sister of adequate communication, our top priority. To achieve this goal demanded the cooperation of a prosperous private sector, honest and efficient government at all levels, and an effective educational program.

In my inaugural address to the Legislature, I said: "Education is the most important function of organized society. ...In all accumulated history, we have only begun to scratch the surface of the human mind. Our new frontiers will be implemented by human ingenuity. We feel that full development of our human resources is the number one challenge of our time."

To improve the effectiveness of our educational programs, we set out to take advantage of every possible grant. At the University of Nebraska in Omaha, Dean Whitson of the Medical College was determined to elevate it from mediocrity to excellence. He went after every available government grant and worked a miracle. In Lincoln, University of Nebraska President Clifford Hardin secured a grant from the Kellogg Corporation in order to build a Center for Continuing Education. This facility houses SAGE (Sharing Across Generations for Enrichment), a member-based program dedicated to providing a variety of life-long educational opportunities for people over the age of fifty. The Center also provides conference facilities for a wide range of study groups.

Through the leadership of Jack McBride of the University's educational television station, and with the cooperation of the private sector and the legislature, we created a statewide Educational Television Network which became a national leader in its field. We built and equipped a new dental school located on the University of Nebraska East Campus in Lincoln. We expanded curriculum and research at both the university and the state colleges. We acquired federally owned surplus land in Clay County and, with the cooperation of the United States Department of Agriculture, the College of Agriculture and the U. S. Congress, we moved the animal research center from its orphan status at Fort Robinson to Clay Center where it was destined to become an international leader.

Much of the progressive legislation I supported was submitted to the legislature by state senators and not historically credited to Morrison. Among these were the Fair Employment Practices Act, Industrial Development Act, Educational Television Network, State Employees Retirement Act providing for pensions, government reorganization, reorganization of state institutions, and the Merit Plan for selection of judges. Much of the Morrison program for progress did not involve legislation but involved mobilizing the private sector. Some examples include creation of the Nebraskaland Foundation, Old West Trail Foundation, Commission on Equal Rights, Committee on Gifted Children, Nebraska Arts Council, Keep Nebraska Beautiful Commission, ethnic festivals such as Czechs Inc., institution of Governor's Luncheons to promote economic development,

Nebraska's first State Promotion to Europe, headed by Maxine.

Governor's Tours to sell Nebraska to the world, foreign promotional tours to sell Nebraska overseas, promotion of People to People Programs, expansion of new uses for agricultural products, and the institution of a tourist promotion program. These are but samples of activity instituted by the Governor which had an impact on history.

Nebraska had a problem that was common to most of the Midwest. Our small towns were being abandoned wholesale. Adequate employment opportunities did not exist for our talented young people. Furthermore, many Nebraskans were not sufficiently aware of opportunities which did exist.

To attack the first problem, we did a number of things. We passed the Industrial Development Act which gave political subdivisions authority to issue revenue bonds with no cost to the taxpayer. We held Governor's Luncheons for CEOs in major cities so we could sell them on investing in Nebraska locations. We sent trade missions to Europe, all of which resulted in more than 140 new industries being located in Nebraska. To accelerate cooperation in the region, we organized the Midwest Governors' Conference to attack our common problems.

Mel Steen, head of the Fish, Game and Parks Commission, sold me on two things: promoting the tourism industry in Nebraska, and improving our environment by using borrow pits along the Interstate as a chain of lakes. We used personnel from his department and the highway department to accomplish these ends.

We launched a tourism industry by sending a mission to Europe headed by First Lady Maxine Morrison. We created the Old West Trail Commission in a cooperative effort with the states of Wyoming, Montana, North Dakota and South Dakota. We set up bus tours of the state for both Nebraskans and foreigners.

To improve our own self-image and knowledge of our assets, we established the Hall of Fame Commission, Community Betterment Contests, the Keep Nebraska Beautiful Commission, and other programs. To address the problem of an aging population, we created the Commission on Aging, the State's first retirement-pension program for all State employees, and the first medical assistance program by passing the Kerr Mills Act. To address the problem of discrimination, the Fair Employment Practices Act was passed and a Commission on the Status of Women was created.

Citizen involvement in the implementation of public policy exploded during this period. The bully pulpit was used to promote year-round use of our school buildings in order to advance learning. We wanted to spot and promote students at an early age who were talented in communication and encourage them to become teachers. Unfortunately, I found some of these ideas either ahead of their time or I was not a good salesman.

In the first year of my administration, I seized on President Kennedy's call for more international contracts by promoting a visit of young German farmers who would live for a while with Nebraska farmers. This promoted better understanding and goodwill at the grassroots level. The program was so successful that the West German government invited me to spend two weeks in Germany as its official guest so I could visit with people in all walks of life - politicians, educators, journalists, business people, laborers, and others - without restriction. An interpreter, transportation and hosting were provided.

Joyce Hall, a native Nebraskan who was father of the greeting card industry,[26] created, through his friend President Eisenhower, the People to People Program in which private citizens from diverse nations and professions could meet with their counterparts to discuss mutual problems and potential solutions. Ike had previously indicated that governments would never end war; the people of the world would some day demand it. Acting on behalf of the former president, Hall commissioned me the first "Ambassador of Good Will" to the Federal Republic of Germany under the Eisenhower program. The experiences in Germany became an invaluable part of my education in many ways.

On arrival at the Bonn Airport, I was greeted by a German who said, "Welcome, Fellow Cornhusker." This man had attended the University of Nebraska. I was escorted to my hotel located on the banks of the Rhine River. All night long a constant flow of riverboats passed by outside my window.

I was taken to many towns and cities. Construction of the Berlin Wall was in its last stages. No German was allowed through the wall. The chief of the Associated Press bureau took me through Check Point Charlie on a visit to East Berlin. The contrast was remarkable. East Berlin was like a cemetery compared to the vibrant and dynamic West.

One night, I crashed a young President Club party at a Berlin Hotel and became acquainted with a couple who spoke good English. She invited me home with them for a cup of coffee and conversation. He had been a member of Hitler's army in Russia. He knew more about American history than most Americans. He posed an interesting question: "Do most Americans know the extent to which the future of democracy and civilization depends on America?"

We could listen to television broadcasts from both East and West Berlin. I knew then that the wall could not wall out communication, that American fear of communism taking over the world was largely a matter of paranoia, and that the ultimate success of communism or capitalism would never be decided on the battlefield or through the arms race.

One of the interesting things during my visit to Munich was the fact that my host had been a young army officer. He showed me pictures of Hitler in review. Here was a young man who was taken out of college to become an officer in Hitler's army. He was sent to Africa and was a part of the Rommel Afrika Korps.[27]

He was wounded in battle. The British captured him and turned him over to the Americans. The Americans sent him back to the United States where, as a prisoner of war, he ended up as manager of a tomato canning factory in Ohio.

This left a lasting impression on me. My host, who was potentially a productive citizen, had contributed to the American economy in a substantial way, yet he was exactly the same man who was obeying Hitler's orders and Rommel's orders as he fought the allies in North Africa. It was exactly the same man; the only difference was the political system under which he was receiving his orders. How could politics ever produce such a bloodbath between people so much alike? How could these wonderful people engage in the Holocaust? I have never experienced a more open society than Germany in the 1960s.

The German Press Association had a cocktail party and President Adenaur's Secretary of State held a luncheon for me. I met Chancellor Kessinger and his cabinet of the State of Baden-Wurttemberg. He was later to become Chancellor of West Germany. We visited the Ruhr Valley, the great industrial district of imperial Germany which fired Imperial Germany's industrial and military might. I went to the Mercedes-Benz plant in Stuttgart. In Stuttgart, I discovered the Brenner Hotel, no doubt named after a distant relative.

As I visited my new-found friends in Berlin and Munich who had served in Hitler's army, I found them to be able, compassionate people, not unlike most Americans. I wondered how such a people could become puppets in the hands of one of the most vicious, cruel dictators in all of human history. I came to the conclusion that no nation has a monopoly on virtue, that modern technology now has made the entire world one community, and that all people must become watchdogs against tyranny in all of its forms. We are as shipmates on a ship called earth. We had better knock down the walls that separate us and learn we have a common human destiny.

I left Cologne, Germany at 9:00 p.m. and was home in bed in Lincoln, Nebraska the same night, knowing the isolation of the world of my childhood was dead forever. Those Germans of World War I, who were painted as demons in our schools, churches, and civic clubs were basically just like us. The ugly wall which the East Berliners built to separate them from the west was harmless compared to the psychological barriers humans build between themselves.

The governorship convinced me of many things. I came to feel our criminal justice system needed a radical overhaul. Far too little was being done to both educate and instill the work ethic in prisoners. We expanded educational programs in the reformatory and did such things as setting up a dental lab in the penitentiary to train lab technicians. Most prisoners will someday be out and will need to live a productive life. Otherwise, they will be back in prison. For me, the wholesale waste of human life was our worst form of waste.

I discovered one of the great opportunities of being governor is to deal with the interrelationship of all levels of government and to become acquainted with people who helped shape the course of history. To me, presidents Truman, Eisenhower, Kennedy, Johnson, Nixon, and Carter became living human beings, not just characters in the news. I am setting forth in other chapters some of my experiences with Kennedy and Johnson with whom I worked as governor.

I first met and became acquainted with Richard Nixon after his defeat by Kennedy and before he was President. He and Pat stayed at the Key Biscayne Hotel in Florida over the New Year's holiday when Nebraska played in the Orange Bowl.

Although Ike's youngest brother, Milton, was a senior the year I was a freshman at Kansas State University, I never met President Eisenhower until 1962. We were attending the annual national Governors' Conference in Hershey, Pennsylvania when the President and Mamie invited us to spend some time with them in their farmhouse adjoining Gettysburg Cemetery. This must be one of the more beautiful spots in this country of ours. The President told us that Mamie picked the site. As I looked out over this cemetery where thousands of young men gave their lives to either end or preserve human slavery and to either preserve or divide this nation, one of the most powerful emotions of my life overtook me. In my mind's eye, I saw a gaunt, sorrowful figure whose shoulders bore the awesome burden of history utter these words:

> "... our fathers brought forth on this continent, a new nation, conceived in Liberty, and dedicated to the proposition that all men are created equal.
>
> Now are we engaged in a great civil war, testing whether that nation, or any other nation so conceived and so dedicated, can long endure. We are met on a great battlefield of that war. We have come to dedicate a portion of that field, as a final resting place for those who here gave their lives that that nation might live. ...
>
> ... It is for us the living, rather, to be dedicated here to the unfinished work [for] which they who fought here ... gave the last full measure of devotion..."[28]

My grandfather's mangled hand flashed back to my consciousness. This had a special meaning when viewed from the home of the man who commanded the allied armies of the world against the forces of human tyranny. If we are to save this precious heritage, every voter and every candidate in this nation must dedicate his or her life to the preservation of this heritage with full knowledge of the obligation we owe to those who preceded us.

Dwight David Eisenhower in many ways was an accident of history. He was at the right place at the right time to become immortal. Product of a very religious family (the River Brethren sect) of German origin, they were peace-loving, anti-war people who settled in Abilene, Kansas. All cadets appointed to West Point receive a free college education. This benefit is provided by the U.S. government to provide well educated officers for the U. S. Army. Thus, by being appointed, Dwight received a free college education. When World War II broke out, he was a Lt. Colonel. Four years later, he was in command of the Allied Armies in Europe. Sincere, approachable, with a total lack of pompousness, but with a personality that inspired confidence, he was a natural leader.

The next time Maxine and I visited with him and Mamie was at a party given by his friend, Joyce Hall. Though commanding the greatest army in human history, he was never totally divorced from his roots. His most profound and prophetic statements are almost never quoted:

> "Our greatest danger is the military industrial complex."

> "Mankind will either end war or war will end mankind."

> "Every weapon we build in final analysis takes food out of the mouth of a hungry child."

These expressions, for me, should be the guideposts for humankind.

It is regrettable more people do not know or have contact with public figures before passing judgment. I first met Governor David Lawrence of Pennsylvania at Hershey. As his companion I visited the historic Crooks County Fair. Meeting him provided a lesson in the dangers of prejudgment. My preformed impression of Lawrence was the one often described by the press: he was the political boss of Pittsburgh. I visualized a self-serving, fat, cigar-smoking tyrant, lining his own pocket. I discovered the opposite to be true. He was an honest, dedicated, humble public servant of good character.

In Nebraska, the governor is chief law enforcement officer of the state. During the governor years, Maxine and I hosted many interesting and famous people. One interesting overnight guest was Claire Booth Luce. She had come close to death while serving as U.S. Ambassador to Italy. Her husband, son of Christian missionaries, and the venerable founder of Time magazine, was violently anti-

Hosted by my friend Governor David Lawrence of Pennsylvania,
I return to Pennsylvania Dutch Country, historic home of the Brenners.

Communist and a strong supporter of Chiang Kai-shek to the bitter end. Two instances in my visits with Mrs. Booth would never appear in the press, but they emphasized the difference between the public persona as revealed in the press and the real person. Most of the public classifies political figures as conservative or liberal. I was standing with Mrs. Booth in the auditorium awaiting her speech when an arch conservative approached her and started giving Hubert Humphrey hell for being a flaming liberal. Mrs. Booth listened for a while, then turned to him and said, "I think Hubert Humphrey is one of the finest men in American politics." Later that evening, I had a long visit with her about international politics and the Vietnam war. She stunned me with this question: "Is it not strange that our nation, which stands for bringing people with a common cultural, ethnic origin and interest together, is fighting a war to keep North Vietnam and South Vietnam separated?" This was a basic mistake which I am sure history will condemn, but a question America's "conservatives" would shrug off as coming from a pro-Communist.

It was a privilege for me to have Chester Bowles as an overnight guest. He was then Under Secretary of State for Latin American Affairs. In discussing our aid program, he stated that we were shipping labor-saving machinery, such as tractors, into Latin America under the aid program, when what they needed was simple tools to make work. Obviously, this policy was designed more as aid to American industry than to alleviate unemployment in Latin America.

After I became Governor and advisor to the Agency for International Development in India where Bowles was ambassador, I enjoyed reading his classified files which should have been in the public domain.

Other visitors to the state while I was Governor stand out in my memory. One was a man named Osmond. He came to the mansion one day with four little boys who were performing at the state fair. They were just starting out and he wanted our opinion as to their talent. This was before Donnie and Marie were born. They were wonderful, but little did I know at the time they were to become world famous entertainers.

Other entertainers who visited the mansion included the cast of Bonanza, George Gobel, Charlton Heston, and others.

My friend, the then Governor of Texas, John Connelly, spent the night.

An annual event sponsored in Broken Bow is a one-box pheasant shoot. I was asked to come there and escort a team of astronauts, including Tom Stafford, Wally Sherar, and Neil Armstrong. Little did I know at the time Neil autographed my program that he would write history as the first human being to walk on the moon, which I watched on television after I left office.

Liz Carpenter, a press secretary in the Johnson Administration, complained that we did not serve liquor in the Governor's mansion. At that time, it was illegal in Nebraska.

There were many interesting and some aggravating experiences. The opportunity to deal with people and the human condition from this vantage point knows no limits. For instance, on one occasion, a little six-year-old girl left a nearby school, walked to the Governor's mansion, and told my wife she wanted a conference with the Governor. The teacher was very angry. Another time, the phone rang late one night and an angry voice on the other end asked me what I was going to do about his kids playing the slot machines in the pool hall in Valley, Nebraska.

In 1966, racial tensions in Omaha were near the boiling point. We expected a riot at any time and were prepared to send in the National Guard immediately to ensure security. The rioters waited to strike until I was in Los Angeles at the National Governors' Conference. Then they set fire to North Omaha. This was in a black neighborhood and most of the damage was to property owned by blacks, which made the action all the more irrational. My Lieutenant Governor, Phil Sorensen, sent the National Guard in immediately. I left the conference, flew back, and took charge.

Between racial conflict and young people starting to rebel against the Vietnam War and public officials generally, my terms as governor had real challenges. The most historic challenge to me was this: Every child must have equal access to develop fully his or her talent and be motivated to accept the responsibility of developing it both for personal fulfillment and enabling society.

In dealing with the public over the years, I have come to believe that our greatest challenge is to improve human awareness - awareness of truth, ourselves, our environment, our opportunities, our responsibilities, the things we have in common, how to communicate, how to motivate, and how to distinguish fact from impression. To meet this challenge, our great educational institutions have a long way to go.

One of the most common comments I heard from people was that there was nothing to do in their community. The truth was that there were hundreds of things to do in every community, but many people were not aware of them.

I noticed how few people knew how to communicate with strangers and, often, even their own friends and relatives. Far too frequently, those who had cultivated the art of communication had no facts to communicate. If we are to meet our obligation to history, we must first link knowledge of truth to the art of communication. To meet this vital need would require the use of every educational building in the state, every week of the year, by teachers who understood the need. Society must learn that teaching is the most important profession because it determines the quality of all others. It holds in its hands the power to motivate and communicate, as well as instruct, the power to build awareness.

My own failure to communicate and motivate was the greatest disappointment of my private and public life. During my three terms as Governor, I discovered many times how the communication of misinformation that bottomed on human emotion rather than fact had tragic consequences. The most serious example was the war in Vietnam. Why did we destroy thousands of lives and consume millions in assets which could have gone a long way in building a better world community? This irrational action was based on the human emotion of fear - fear that this was a monolithic communist movement by the USSR, the Peoples Republic of China, plus North Vietnam to take over South Asia and then move on to the west.

The facts were that the USSR, the Peoples Republic of China, and North Vietnam were enemies, not confederates. On one occasion, the President sent Air Force One to pick up the governors at a national conference and take us to Washington to be briefed by him, the Secretary of State, Secretary of Defense and others, all of which, as Secretary McNamara later pointed out, was unjustified by facts. The governors were to be briefed on our objectives in the Vietnam War to provide public support for our military action. We were told that North Vietnam was a part of a monolithic communist conspiracy among North Vietnam, China and the Soviet Union to take over Southeast Asia as a step toward world domination and that our purpose was to punish North Vietnam so that it would withdraw from South Vietnam and thus end the threat to our security.

The facts were that North Vietnam and China were historic enemies and that China and the Soviet Union had thousands of miles of fortified border because they were enemies who distrusted each other. North Vietnam only wanted to unite the country as agreed to when it was originally separated. North Vietnam erroneously thought the United States was out to destroy communism and impose capitalism on its people against their will.

On the way to that conference, I had an interesting conversation with my seat mate, Governor George Wallace of Alabama. He brought up the subject of racial segregation and discrimination. He told me that the reason for segregation was the difference in the moral standards of the two races. He cited an example of a little thirteen-year-old black girl who became pregnant. She was brought to the school administrator who asked how this had happened. The girl giggled and replied that it happened during recess. He told me that people who had this attitude toward sex could not be mixed with white children. This illustrated another weakness in human conclusions. We over-generalize from a specific. We judge groups by the conduct of one individual within the group. My reply to Governor Wallace was, "I believe in discrimination based on individual worth and qualifications and not that of the group. I do not believe everybody should be president of the bank, school superintendent, elected to Phi Beta Kappa or governor, but rather those honors should be based on individual worth." I asked him why he would associate socially with an immoral white man and not a moral black man to which he replied, "That would be discrimination between Negroes." He later admitted publicly that he was wrong.

Far too much of our public action is based on the communication of misinformation. When I was Governor, the Governor was ex-officio chairman of the Pardons as well as the Parole Board. On one occasion, a man from Death Row appeared before us on petition to have his death sentence commuted to life imprisonment. Our investigation disclosed that the reason the jury recommended death rather than life imprisonment was based on false information. They were told that if they gave him life, he would be paroled out in a few years and repeat his crime of murder. What the jury did not know was that in fact, never in Nebraska's hundred year history had a convicted murderer been paroled out and thereafter committed another murder. The verdict had been based on false information and the irrational emotion of fear. We commuted the sentence to life imprisonment.

The warehousing of prisoners, rather than attacking the causes of crime and using rational methods of rehabilitation, are a blight on our whole criminal justice system. Both government and education face a great challenge in the area of human conduct. My efforts toward reform have been both inadequate and ineffective. At age 95, I wish I had the energy, resources, and time to marshal the facts upon which to base a complete overhaul of our whole approach to criminal conduct.

26 Joyce Hall was founder of Hallmark Cards.

27 Erwin Rommel was Hitler's brilliant field marshal in Africa during World War II. Known as the "Desert Fox" for his surprise attacks on enemy troops, and winner of numerous important battles, he eventually came to understand the futility of Hitler's ability to win the war and tried to convince Hitler of this to no avail.

In the spring of 1944, Rommel was approached by conspirators who wanted to overthrow and assassinate Hitler. Rommel was a professional soldier, not a political personage. Murder was not to his liking, so he refused to take part in the plot. In July 1944, British fighter-bombers forced Rommel's car off the road seriously injuring him. Shortly after, the conspirators failed in an attempt on Hitler's life. Unfortunately, Rommel's name became publicly connected with them. Since Rommel had been a popular German officer and Hitler did not want any public appearance of discord between them, he sent two generals to Rommel who gave him poison with the suggestion that he should take it to avoid ruining his family's name in a trial. On October 14, 1944, Rommel took the poison.

28 Abraham Lincoln, *The Gettysburg Address*, November 19, 1863.

Trade Mission

I flew to Washington on October 13, 1965 where I was briefed by two cabinet members and other people. I sat in the United States Senate chamber for a while, steeped in the glow of history, and in my mind's eye, I saw the debates of past statesmen Webster, Clay, Calhoon, Norris, and LaFollette. Their voices had given way to the voices of Mansfield, Kennedy, and a host of others. Historic votes were being taken there on the Senate floor.

From this scene and background I set off with my fellow Nebraskans on a trade mission to Europe. We flew from Washington's Dulles Airport to New York, Boston, Newfoundland, missed the coast of Greenland, and then over Ireland and on into London. On the way to London that night, my mind went back to my horse and buggy days. What a revolution had taken place in transportation and communication during my lifetime, more than all of the thousands of years of human existence before my birth.

I noticed that the same North Star was there that had shone on mankind since he first appeared on this planet and long before. It had been here since time began, if time had a beginning. I knew that somewhere out there was a purpose known to God alone. As I pondered the fleeting scene of man's appearance on this earth, a silver light soon appeared in the north, gradually giving way to red; then appeared the sun.

The stars were gone and we were in London. At the terminal, I was met by William R. Rusch, Commercial Attaché of the American Embassy, and Ed Borsch of the American Trade Commission. London was still a city of importance but was no longer the center of the universe it had been for half a thousand years or more. Still, it was an important financial, commercial, and political hub for the world.

As our plane descended out of the sky, the panorama of history unfolded in my mind. The Celts, Anglos, Saxons, Roman conquerors, and William the Conqueror stood before me in my mind's eye. I envisioned King John, the Magna

Carta, and Runnemede on the banks of the Thames River. Great Britain gave us our legacy of the common law. There was Churchill, the indomitable spirit of the British people destined to rule the world at one time in human history. My mind fleetingly passed by Shakespeare, Byron, Keats, and Dickens, leaving their writing for generations yet unborn. I was tired after the night on the plane, but not too tired to see the glow of history as it cast its shadow onto today and tomorrow.

As I stood in Westminster Abbey, I first thought of it as ancient hallowed ground. I stood there and watched the pages of history fly past me. I looked at the throne where modern kings of England had assumed the ceremony of coronation. What a strange mixture in this room of history - a mixture of death, religion, culture, and politics. I stood on top of the grave of Charles Darwin, who gave us a new theory about the origin of the species, including man. The bodies of Lord Tennyson, Ben Johnson, William Wordsworth, and many other literary giants lay moldering under these marble slabs. The words they wrote will live on and enrich the lives of men and women forever. I wondered what role I might have to play, what of importance could I say that could contribute something to this current humanity that flows through the corridors of time.

Before I started on this trip, I attended a meeting of the National Postmasters held in Nebraska. My dinner partner was James A. Farley, who wrote an important chapter in the history of our own nation. Farley managed President Roosevelt's first campaign for the presidency. He had served as President of the Coca-Cola Export Company since leaving politics. I told him I was going to leave early because I was going to Europe. He inquired about my mission and asked me a number of questions. He asked if I would like to have a limousine and a driver at my disposal in London who would take me anywhere in England. I thought what a privilege, as there was no conflict of interest here. Coca-Cola had never asked me for a favor and never would. So I said I would be glad to accept. He also asked me if I had ever met Max Smelling, who was living in Hamburg, and I said no. He asked me if I would like to meet him, and I said I certainly would. Farley set up arrangements for me to have dinner with Smelling sometime when I was in Hamburg.

Farley first knew Max when he was Boxing Commissioner of the State of New York. After the war, Max was a citizen of Nazi Germany without funds for his support and without employment, so Farley had given Max the Coca-Cola franchise in Hamburg, a gift worth more than a million dollars.

In London, I took advantage of the limousine and chauffeur to take another member of the delegation and me to Stratford on Avon, the setting where Shakespeare had composed his immortal plays and poetry. We also saw the grave of Sir Winston Churchill in the small village where he had lived. Then we went

A post mortem visit with Churchhill.

to Runnemede, that beautiful spot on the banks of the Thames River where the Magna Carta became a reality.

As I visited Runnemede, I thought about our own country and its revolution to throw off the power of kings. I thought what an impact the Magna Carta had made on the world. I stood there reliving the events which were stepping-stones toward the limited power of emperors and the state over human life. I looked around and saw a monument that had been built to the memory of John F. Kennedy, a man of Irish extraction whose ancestors had fought with the British over the centuries, the man I had met in Lincoln, Nebraska, the man I had been with on his wedding anniversary, the man who was in many ways my inspiration in politics. There was his monument, erected overlooking that wonderfully beautiful spot at Runnemede, where the power of the emperors, where the power for government over every detail of human life was curtailed. That scene and those memories were to become a part of my life forever.

In rapid succession, I had lunch with Lawrence Youngman. Then followed a conference with Bruce, our Ambassador to Great Britain, at the American Embassy. I also met at the American Embassy with Harold E. Hall, Counselor for Commercial Affairs. His wife was related to, and was a good friend of, the Neville family in North Platte, Nebraska. Hall had lunch with me the day before with Mr. Gillan, President of the Ford Motor Company in Britain and a prominent member of Parliament. I would have hated to miss this.

I had an appointment with Mr. James Haug, Secretary of the Minister of Agriculture and a member of Parliament. Mr. Emil Kelisch, Executive Director of the American Chamber of Commerce, called and asked me to have lunch with him at the famous American Club. Here, I met Beverly Miller, head of the American Travel Service, who had met with my wife when she led the delegation of Nebraskans on a Promote Nebraska trip in Europe. Miller praised Maxine and told of the huge impact she had when she was there.

I also met with Warren Pearl, a leading London insurance man, and James Stillwell, President of the American Club. Included at the lunch was William Lyons, Director of Pan American Airlines and President of American Chamber of Commerce in London. We also had lunch with William Fitzgerald, Manager of Special Sales for Pan American. We discussed problems and possibilities of the expansion of beef imports from Nebraska to Britain.

The afternoon was a thrilling experience. Mr. Bill Rusch took me first to the famous Lincoln's Inn and then to the Middle Temple. As a lawyer, I had long revered these Historic Inns of the Court of London that were built before Columbus discovered America. All barristers in the United Kingdom must be members and be called to practice by one of the Inns.

We were met at the Middle Temple by Derek Scuchey. We saw many coats of arms going back to the Middle Ages. We saw the table made from timbers taken from Sir Francis Drake's ship. In this building, Shakespeare's *Twelfth Night* was first produced, and it is thought that the actor himself appeared in the cast.

Then we attended a trial complete with the judge, the wig, the barristers and robe of course. It was a divorce case, not too different from our own. The barristers both had a tape recorder and a shorthand reporter took notes during the trial.

A majority of my time spent in England up to this point had been primarily cultural in nature. My vision of these trade missions was both cultural and economic. In many respects, the two are intertwined. I think the promotion of trade and tourism is facilitated by a better understanding and appreciation of the culture of our trading partners. With this in mind, we spent part of the time in cultural activities but, mostly, our time was spent in discussing economic opportunities, trade possibilities, and the expansion of tourism, trade, and investments.

In conversations with Mr. Haug, the Minister of Agriculture, and other people involved in the development of this phase of our economy, we were not unmindful of the fact that most of our breeds of livestock, practically all of them, originated in western Europe. Our principal beef breeds of cattle - Herefords, Aberdeen Angus, and Shorthorns - originated in Great Britain. All of our other dairy cattle, and most of our other breeds of livestock, originated in western Europe.

Our interchange of information, including talk about trade possibilities and the potential of American research, has great value, not only for Nebraska and the heart of our agricultural region, but for the American economy generally. It also has an immense role to play in the progress of agriculture in western Europe.

A major part of our trade mission was to center out of Hamburg, Germany, Schleswig-Holstein, Rotterdam, and Paris. First, we landed in beautiful Hamburg, which is located on the Lake of Ulster. This city has a unique history. It became a part of the German Empire, but for many years prior to that, Hamburg was a city/state of its own, a part of the Hanseatic League.[29] It became one of the world's great seaports. The Hanseatic League itself centered on the Baltic and from thence out to the Atlantic. This became an immense center of world trade.

Our delegation was met by the mayor and city officials who accorded us a royal welcome to Hamburg. We contacted people in many areas of commerce and culture in the city with the full support and cooperation of the city government. Hamburg held not only an interest for me and the rest of the delegation in discussing trade policies, but it presented interesting European investment possibilities in Nebraska.

We had, in Lincoln particularly, a thriving interest in aviation. Charles Lindbergh took his first flying lessons in Lincoln. Duncan Aviation, based in

Lincoln, had tremendous potential in the whole national-international market. It was a center for executive aircraft. We had entertained Bill Lair and some of his people in Lincoln while they set up a liaison between the Lair Manufacturing Company, which was a principal maker of executive aircraft, and the Duncan Aviation and local aviation interests. While in Hamburg, I contacted a manufacturer of executive aircraft who was entering the market with a completely new airplane design. During my conversations with the executives of this company, they were trying out a new model of their aircraft and were going on a test run to Stuttgart from Hamburg. They asked me to go along as their guest, which I did. This in many ways was foolhardy, but we took off and flew to Stuttgart and back.

The American council had a reception for our delegation at the Cosmopolitan Club. This club is located on the Alster, and the reflection of the city lights across the water is a magnificent sight. German businessmen attended this reception and I kept a list of these names. We met a Swiss family there at this reception, and I set up a meeting with them for the next day. Both in England and in Hamburg, our delegation spread out and made many valuable contacts. Phil Anderson in our delegation signed a new contract in Lincoln and another one in Hamburg.

The next morning, we attended another conference on animal feeds conducted by Dr. Giehart Pesht. We discussed imports we found to be very expensive. Our work in Hamburg overlapped with a visit to Schleswig-Holstein. That is a state of Germany which is well known in many phases of agriculture and was the place where the Holstein breed originated. We attended a conference here conducted by Alan Freck, the Agricultural Officer for the American Council. Here, we met our host, Herman Feaux DeArlaroix, a German farmer whose ancestors came from France. This man was president of the feed industry of West Germany. His farm was a magnificent old brick mansion, high above the beautiful meadows surrounded by trees. Herman provided us with refreshments and took us on a tour of his farm. The dairy barn housed about one hundred cows which were enclosed all winter. The milk was conducted from a barn by overhead pipes. It passed through a chilling room where it was prepared for market. What a contrast to the old Brenner farm!

From the dairy barn, we went to the hog barn, which was by far the most progressive means of housing hogs I have ever seen. This particular barn housed approximately two hundred hogs with about ten to a compartment. Each compartment had two parts, one where the hogs lived, and the other where the hogs went to relieve themselves and defecate. This is the first time in my life I have experienced housebred hogs as a part of the hog industry. This farm was a great example of modern farming at its best. The farm contained about 1,400 acres and had approximately sixteen employees.

From this farm, we went to the factory and experiment station of one of

A visit to East Berlin after Destalinization in 1961.

Germany's largest manufacturers of feed supplement. This fast growing organization employed seven hundred salesman on the road to market their products. Their fruit supplement was a mixture designed to be used with existing feed and to balance the animals' diet. The company was twenty-seven years old. It used fifteen percent of all the antibiotics in the German feed industry. Most of its chemicals and antibiotics were imported from the United States and used in the food supplement. The owner was thinking about taking over the SPF program for hogs, which program was developed in Nebraska.

Rotterdam, located at the mouth of the Rhine River, is the world's greatest seaport and has been for many years. It was completely bombed out during the Second World War. Rotterdam recovered. The people of Rotterdam made rebuilding the seaport their first priority after the war. When one approaches the port, it looks like a group of concentrated oil derricks. These derricks transfer cargo from ocean liners from all over the world to trucks or vice versa. It is a magnificent sight to behold and is an inspiration for anybody interested in international trade and commerce. In Rotterdam, the Nebraska Wheat Commission had established headquarters.

I spent that night with the President and Secretary of the Bonn Rotary Club as their guest. This impressed me with the role that this great international service club can play in better human understanding. The Secretary of the Bonn Rotary Club was also the Director of the Dresden Bank. He was a friend of Kaiser Wilhelm and one of the Kaiser's sons. This was the same Kaiser who was despised in America during the First World War and who was the subject of the movie called *The Kaiser, the Beast of Berlin*. Before I left, the Secretary gave me a picture of Frederick the Great of Germany with an inscribed message from him on the back of the picture.

One night I stayed at a beautiful hotel in the industrial city of Dusseldorf, which in 1961 was a city of 750,000 people. On the day of the trade fair, we looked over exhibits from various countries. There were over two thousand models and women's clothes on exhibit from all over the world. The hotel in Dusseldorf had, I think, the most beautiful bathroom fixtures I have ever seen.

From Dusseldorf, we went to Cologne where we visited the famous cathedral, the construction of which was commenced in the thirteenth century. I was in the city of Bonn a number of times. One time, I had a conference with the foreign minister of the federal government of Bonn, Carl Gunther VonHaase. He was a brilliant young man who discussed foreign policy with us without inhibitions. He admitted the guilt of Germany under Hitler. He analyzed the communist worldwide movement from his point of view.

We had a conference with Herb Franz Joseph Wuermeling, federal minister of youth, and his staff. This was one of the most interesting conferences in all my stay in Germany and was quite revealing in its information. It took place in the minister's office. We discussed the German school system through our interpreter, Christina Wills. At that time, the primary school system was controlled by the states or government. It consisted of eight to ten years of school, depending upon the state. At the end of the fourth year of school those students who desired to enter the gymnasium, or college preparatory school, did so. They left elementary school then for the gymnasium. Other students continued for the eight or ten years, at the end of which they attended a trade school if they wished. Only the universities or technical colleges received any money from the federal government. Over half of the state government taxes went for education. They subsidized both public and church schools. With reference to kids who are at risk with behavioral problems, if the kids are not too bad, they are left in school under the private tutoring of a parole officer who visits with the youngster and analyzes his problems and helps him with them. I think we have a great deal to learn in Nebraska and in America generally from this approach to juvenile delinquency.

I also learned that the federal government subsidized private political clubs which taught their party policies to encourage mass participation in politics and policy formulations.

Government control over agriculture was interesting. Wheat price was established by the German government. It was imported by the government at world price and sold at a fixed price. The government skimmed off the difference. This is called skimming instead of a tariff. They thought the common market would probably hurt import of American agricultural products into Germany.

Labor was in short supply in Germany. Six thousand Italians, Spaniards, and Greeks were imported for labor. These people sent money home and returned to their home country when their work was over.

We toured the Ruhr Basin, which is one of the most heavily industrialized regions of the world. We visited with the cattle people in the farm country of Bavaria. One thing that impressed me about the cattle market in Bavaria was that old bulls brought a higher price than young animals.

We toured the Mercedes-Benz plant in Stutgaard, went to the top of the needle, and spent some time becoming acquainted with this part of Germany. Probably my middle name and my maternal grandfather's name originated here.

I returned to Cologne and departed from there at 9:00 p.m. knowing I would be home in bed in Lincoln, Nebraska that same night.

Among the many things that I learned as governor was that the vast number of public servants who work hard to make life better for all of us receive little publicity and are largely unknown. These include highway patrolmen, electric and telephone lineman, clerks, mailmen, nurses, and a host of others.

My administration could never have been successful in bringing many new industries into the state affording employment opportunities for thousands of people except for the work and leadership of David Osterhoudt. He never sought recognition for himself, but worked tirelessly in contacting business people all over America, attending trade fairs, setting up contacts and Governor's Luncheons to sell Nebraska.

Many people came to me with ideas which had potential but needed promotion. Among them was a man who was convinced children needed a program to help the environment and promote the planting of precious walnut trees, which were all but extinct. He had an idea called "Squire P. Squirrel." Black walnuts were distributed to school kids to take home and plant. The man had a nervous breakdown after a year or two of the program and it died for want of leadership.

Another idea was the "Inventors' Congress." Many great ideas are never implemented because the inventor, promoter, industrialist, and banker never get together. Such a congress afforded this opportunity.

During my years as governor, many wonderful things happened to our family. Maxine was elected Chairman of the Governor's Wives of the United States in an attempt to get first ladies involved in public policy and service. Our oldest son, Frank Jr. (Biff), graduated from law school in Denver, went to work for McGinley, Lane in Ogallala, and was then recruited by future Judge Don Lay to join the Eisenstat law firm in Omaha. Our second son, David Jon, married Jerry Jones of Beaumont, Texas and our daughter married Dr. Ben Galloway. The children and their families gave my conscious life a new dimension.

In the latter part of my third term, I had several options: run for a fourth term; contest U.S. Senator Carl Curtis for his senate seat with the understanding that if I were not successful, I would be appointed to the 8th Circuit Court of Appeals; enter private law practice with my son in Omaha; or resume law practice in Lincoln.

In the last year of my service as Governor - the last year of my third term - a vacancy occurred in the 8th Circuit Court of Appeals. Being a lawyer deeply interested in the administration of justice, it occurred to me that I would like an appointment as a judge of this court. I flew into Washington and had an appointment to meet with President Johnson to discuss this with him. He listened to me attentively. He indicated he would like me to seek the Senate seat which had been occupied for many years by Republican Carl Curtis. He asked me if I thought it was possible for me to win the election or to defeat Senator Curtis. My own ego, I guess, got the best of me for the moment. I indicated that I thought I could.

Before I left for home, I met with Larry O'Brien, the close friend and supporter of President Kennedy who had continued on with the Johnson staff. He indicated to me that federal judges were a dime a dozen and emphasized the importance of being in the United States Senate.

After I returned home, I received a call from an attorney named White who was then on the President's staff. Attorney White said it was his understanding the President would hold the appointment until after the election.

I hate public policy based on polls, but for my own information, I had a poll done by one of the top national organizations. It showed that if I ran for a fourth term as governor, I would be elected overwhelmingly. If I ran for the Senate, I would be defeated badly by Senator Curtis. Nevertheless, I had a deep feeling that I could never accomplish what I thought needed to be done without the power of the U.S. government. I had seen my friend, Carl, vote against confirmation of the Atmospheric Test Ban Treaty when ending this testing was essential to stop serious pollution of the atmosphere as far away as Nebraska. He had voted against such things as the Mental Health Act and federal aid to education acts which I deemed essential to Nebraska and the nation's educational system. I felt that the federal government was essential to stop waste of our human and material resources.

I decided to become a candidate for the United States Senate and delivered a speech in which I outlined the reasons for my decision:

> "It is my prayer that this day live forever in the history of the state, not as a day when one man announced his decision as to what public office he would seek, but as the day of decision for people of a great state as to the direction of their historic movement. It is my ambition that Nebraska become a flagship in the American fleet of states.
>
> We meet here today in America's only unicameral legislative chamber on land President Jefferson made a part of the American union. In a nation whose unity was purchased by the blood of Lincoln and the men of his time - enhanced, preserved, and protected by the life and vision of our fathers. Yesterday, the federal court put its stamp of approval on Nebraska's historic reapportionment. Yesterday, I witnessed the rapid loss of our soil and water which this nation must have to preserve and enhance its strength for the job ahead.
>
> Since I have been your Governor, I have seen, as you have, only feeble attempts made to check the erosion of either our material or human resources. This cannot be done without the full utilization of the resources of the federal government.

I have heard the statesmen who represent us in the senate denounce the power of the federal government rather than outline programs for a self-reliant people of vision to use this power as a tool in their hand to write history as it must be written in our time.

I have seen, as you have, for thirty years, production control of foodstuffs in the face of a hungry world. Expanded world trade must end this stumbling block to economic progress.

I have seen, as you have, a seat in the United States Senate used to preach hate of the President and those with whom we disagree rather than the writing of a blueprint for dynamic action.

We live in an explosive, dangerous and revolutionary period of world history where we recognize that ignorance, hatred, starvation, disease, and erosion are the basic enemies of mankind and all of us must unite to combat them, if we are to survive. Reason and not passion must guide us in the perilous journey ahead.

I have heard, as you have, our seat in the United States Senate used as a forum to divide our strength rather than as a platform from which to lead the nation to new dimensions of positive attainment.

The programs which are making Nebraska a leader among the states are well launched. Other men carry them forward.

The full development of our human and natural resources cannot be accomplished without the full utilization of the resources of the federal government.

This can and must be done, not by allowing this power to become the master and enslaver of men, but as a powerful tool in the hands of responsible self-reliant men to achieve their historic destiny.

Ignorance, hatred, starvation, greed, disease and erosion are the links in the chain which enslave mankind. On the eye of Lincoln's birthday, I call upon you, my fellow Nebraskans, not to fight each other, but to achieve new degrees of freedom and emancipation from man's historic enemies. This is the challenge of emancipation for our time.

We can never achieve freedom until men are emancipated from this bondage. It can be done only by people determined to become masters of government and not its slaves.

To attain this new emancipation, I invite all of you who will not sacrifice adventure for comfort, work for idleness, or freedom

The First Lady of the United States is our overnight guest.

for security to become partners with me in this undertaking.

This cannot be done without a positive voice in the United States Senate. This cannot be done without full partnership of private business, local, state and national government.

It was Abraham Lincoln who charted our course for federal aid to education in the Morrill Act and gave this nation a vision of universal human freedom and the quality of the American union. I invite the political heirs of Lincoln and those of Jefferson who believe the historic role of this nation is to teach mankind and not to destroy it to join with me in the most historic encounter in the history of this state between two opposing schools of thought in the role we must play in writing the history of our time."

During this campaign the First Lady of the United States, Lady Bird Johnson, came to Lincoln as the guest of Nebraskaland Days, and spent the day at the Governor's mansion in Lincoln. Nebraskaland Days were set up as festivities to celebrate the history and heritage of our state. Before moving to North Platte, the parade and ceremony took place in Lincoln. It was quite a festive occasion. Lady

Bird rode with me and my grandson, John Morrison, in the parade. During the afternoon, a secret service man approached us and said that a line of thunderstorms had appeared between Lincoln, Nebraska and Austin, Texas. The First Lady was hesitant to fly in turbulent weather, so arrangements were made for her that night with us at the Governor's mansion. This necessitated the secret service invading every precinct of the Governor's mansion, all of the clothes closets, all of the bedrooms, and all of the surrounding grounds.

Late that night, I continued to have a one-on-one conversation with the First Lady who had done so much to handle her responsibilities with dignity. I shared with her a deep concern for beautifying and making our environment more inspiring. Her primary interest in furthering that end was the promotion of our appreciation for wildflowers. All of this was mixed in with public policy and the reality of politics.

The campaign continued. I was defeated in the election. The interesting thing is that my opponent, Senator Curtis, had supported the Vietnam War while I had little to do with it. I reaped the harvest of the unpopularity of the war which was developing at that time.

My failure to accept appointment to the 8th U.S. Circuit Court of Appeals was probably partly due to the thrill of practicing law with my son in Omaha. So Maxine and I packed our clothes and moved to a high-rise apartment in downtown Omaha known as the Longo. I joined the law firm of Eisenstat, Morrison, Higgins, Miller, and Morrison.

29 The Hanseatic League was formed in the thirteenth century as an alliance of German merchants who traveled together for safety and convenience. The League in one form or another lasted nearly five centuries.

Life in Omaha

I knew Dr. Longo. As a physician, he wanted his monument to be an attractive high-rise apartment house in downtown Omaha. He built one. I had attended the dedication not knowing that I would someday live there. We moved into a lovely apartment on the 10th floor, looking out over the Missouri River and Council Bluffs. On these Bluffs, Abraham Lincoln had stood and dreamed of a day when a railroad would cross the river here and proceed west, binding this continent together as one nation. He never lived to see that become a reality, but it did. When built, it followed the great Platte River Road west and laid the foundation for converting a small nation into the great superpower it is today.

I had difficulty adjusting to the law practice at first. I had lost my clients to become Governor. To some degree, I had also lost my effectiveness in the court-room. People thought of me as a politician, not a lawyer. Notwithstanding this fact, my son and I tried some celebrated cases. A small percentage of people think of all politicians as dishonest, regardless of how honest and truthful they may be. One or two of these on a jury can be a disaster. I discovered I had paid a heavy price for public service.

We had moved to Omaha in January of 1967, the month I left office. The next year, our son, Biff, persuaded Maxine to run for Congress. He managed a hard fought campaign in the Democratic primary and defeated a very able popular County Commissioner, Jack Cavanaugh. In the general election she was pitted against longtime Congressman Glenn Cunningham, who had lost his effective-ness because of ill health and an alleged drinking problem.

This was the year Hubert Humphrey won the Democratic nomination for President after a bruising convention battle in Chicago where the Daly police were accused of brutality. Governor George Wallace left the Democratic party and ran for the presidency representing the American Independent Party.[30] He carried five southern states winning almost ten million votes. It appeared no candidate might get a majority and the election would be thrown into the House of Representatives.

Richard Nixon was the Republican nominee. Nixon was more popular in Nebraska than any of the other states so to ensure his election was top priority for Nebraska Republicans. This solidified the Nebraska Republicans. In the minds of Republican leaders, they could not risk losing a seat in Congress. Both Republican U.S. senators were put on television to remind voters that the welfare of the nation depended on Nixon's election. The fact that the election might end up in Congress made voting for Cunningham imperative. Even the endorsement of the *Omaha World-Herald*, which seldom endorsed a Democrat, was not enough to overcome the Nixon groundswell. Biff took the election as an insult to his mother and good government. He never quite reconciled himself to the Omaha voters.

I became increasingly concerned about the wisdom of our war in Vietnam. Johnson, Humphrey, and Nixon were all strong supporters of the war. I asked the government to send me to Vietnam to better understand what was going on then, but they refused. They said I could do more good by going to India so I was sent there as an advisor to the Agency for International Development. My experiences in India were to change my thinking on global matters and American foreign policy forever. In India I saw with my own eyes the collision between modern technology and a culture, economy, agriculture, and traditions which had existed for thousands of years.

Communism was born in the mind of Karl Marx, who lived in industrialized Germany and saw workers exploited by greedy capitalism. He thought capitalism, by its very nature, created a modern kind of industrial slavery and the only remedy was for the government to own and operate all means of production. The USSR became the power base of communism. The U.S. became the power base of capitalism. Each had a mortal fear of the other. Both superpowers sought to convert the other nations to their point of view with propaganda, domestic civilian and military aid such as weapons and military training and, in some cases, such as Vietnam American military involvement.

India refused to become allied with either side. Indian leaders maintained vigorous trade relations with the USSR, took Russian aid, allowed the USSR to circulate anti-American propaganda, let the Communists become a political party in India, and at the same time, milked the U.S. for all the aid and technology it was willing to give. Neither country was allowed military bases or any kind of military action. The battle was to be political and at the ballot box.

Fortunately, during the Eisenhower administration Congress passed the 480 Program which allowed us to get rid of surplus wheat by shipping it to food deficit nations such as India. In the case of India, the purchase money was to be used to build State Agricultural Universities modeled after our Land Grant College Act. This, coupled with research from the Rockefeller and Ford Foundations, converted India from food deficit and famine to a food exporting nation.

In India, all drinking water was polluted. Sanitary sewers were all but nonexistent. The rodents were eating more wheat than we were shipping in.

The United States had taken one giant step toward bringing India into the 20th century when it decided to use 480 Funds to establish what we knew as land grant colleges. This made a three-pronged attack on ignorance through research, demonstration, and instruction. Had we taken these additional steps, communism would have died on the vine. Any attorney familiar with creating political subdivisions and farmers' co-ops, knows that financing improvement districts. Coupled with some engineering advice and modern banking practices, the Indians could have been taught how to create sanitary districts by issuing bonds to pay for sewers and sewage plants where enough sanitized fertilizer would have been recovered to pay for the bonds. Farmers' co-ops could have been created to build rodent-proof storage facilities as contrasted to sheds piled with wheat-filled gunny sacks which furnished a buffet for rats. Irrigation districts could have been created as a substitute for the primitive pump driven by a water buffalo. Any intelligent high school kid should have been able to figure this out, but the greatest brains assembled in Washington could not. They were spending billions in dropping bombs on poverty-riddled peasants in rice paddies in Vietnam.

India was obviously over-populated. Rotary clubs set up stations offering free vasectomies. The government had a vast billboard campaign to limit families to three children. The United States was spending millions to educate Indians on family planning and birth control. I was not in India long before I learned these programs were ineffective. Educated wealthy people in India were not having too many children; it was only the poverty stricken and uneducated whose standard of living was such that children were an economic asset rather than liability. The answer was to reduce poverty and increase education.

I was briefed in Washington by the State Department for days before going to India. I was told that to do physical work in India was to lose credibility as an authority, that educated people did no physical work. I should even let others carry my suitcase.

My first assignment was to visit the new Agricultural University at Pant Nager. I visited a faculty meeting where I met the Dean of the Veterinary Department. He informed me that he held clinics out in the country where he administered treatment to sick animals as both an extension and teaching program for his students. I told him I would like to go along. About six the next morning, an old pickup pulled in front of the house where I was staying and the driver honked the horn. I went out to the old pickup and found the veterinarian dressed in overalls.

Much to my consternation, I discovered it was not a laborer but the Dean himself who took me to the clinic where he performed the physical work of dealing with the animals. This native Indian had a string of degrees from a prestigious university and engaged in plenty of physical work. So much for the experts in the State Department.

I visited the State Universities at Hyderabad and Bangalore. At once, I was greeted by the Indian President of one of these universities with, "You made me an admiral in the Nebraska Navy." The mythical land-locked Nebraska Navy was created some fifty years ago to honor distinguished people.

Christian missionaries had been attempting to convert Indian people to Christianity for over fifteen hundred years with little success. In Bangalore, I found a Catholic priest who took a different approach. He was born and grew up in Madrass in southern India. He decided to found a Catholic seminary where young men would work for their education. He bought a farm near Bangalore and converted it into a strictly modern dairy. He said he figured if they wanted to worship a cow, they should have a worthy cow. The church gave him some money. The U.S. loaned him an old cargo plane. He came to the United States, bought a first-grade registered Holstein bull and some top Holstein milk cows and took off for Bangalore. The students operated the farm and received their education. I have never seen a more modern dairy. This was a perfect example of what religion, the private sector, and government can do by working intelligently together.

Maxine was in the heat of her campaign for Congress. My friend, Chester Bowles, was U.S. Ambassador to India. Indira Gandhi was Prime Minister and head of the India government. India was by far the most populous democracy on earth. Maxine wanted to come to India and interview her. I asked the Colgate graduate who was the Ambassador's Chief of Staff to set it up. He said he would, but it would do no good. He described the Prime Minister as aloof, someone who would sit behind her desk and answer no questions. He said Maxine's visit would be a waste of time. Maxine came anyway. Chester Bowles said he and his wife were going back to the states for a visit and asked Maxine and me to live in the Embassy indefinitely.

When the time arrived to visit the Prime Minister, the Chief of Staff informed us that he had never met the Prime Minister and asked if he could go along. When we entered the Prime Minister's office, we found her to be exactly the opposite of what we had been told officially. She jumped up from her desk, came to the door to welcome us, engaged in lively conversation, and was familiar with the role Senator Norris from Nebraska had played in supporting Indian independence. She never failed to answer a barrage of questions we threw at her. She told us that India did not want American charity, but did want us to share our know-how and expertise with her country. She was generous with her time and never once did

*Maxine and I confer with Prime Minister Gandhi
in her office in New Delhi, India.*

anyone interrupt or shorten our visit. When we excused ourselves and left, a U.S. Information Officer told us that no American had ever spent that much time in the Prime Minister's office. I think she knew more about America than most Americans. Maxine asked her how she campaigned for office as a woman, and she replied, "Just like a man." I wondered in this information age why so much of our policy is founded on misinformation.

The United States Information Service asked me to talk to Rotary Clubs without restriction on subject matter. One of my interesting experiences was to talk for the first joint banquet of the Rotary and Lion's Clubs of Amritsar in northwest India near the Pakistani border. It was the birthplace of the Seik religion. I was guest in the home of a prominent dye manufacturer whose lifestyle was not unlike that of any industrialist in America.

I had gradually assumed a dual role in India as a lecturer for the United States Information Service and an advisor to the Agency for International Development. It was during this period I received news that was to change the history of my country. Wire services carried the news that Bobby Kennedy had carried the California primary, which meant he was on his way to capturing the Democratic nomination for President and would be the odds-on favorite to be elected over Nixon. Then the news came that he had been assassinated. I received an invitation to return for his funeral, but did not have time to make the arrangements. Kennedy had pledged to stop the war in Vietnam. Had he not been assassinated, we would have saved billions of dollars and thousands of lives. There would have been no Watergate, no fiasco at the Democratic convention in Chicago, and Maxine Morrison would probably have been elected to Congress.

In India, I was impressed with the fact that in that part of the world, modern technology existed side by side with ancient customs. As I was traveling in a rural area one day, I saw a farmer with a hand plow pulled by a water buffalo while a jet airplane was flying overhead.

I was impressed by the fact that historically, India had periodically suffered from famine and food shortages. Mother nature made the subcontinent subject to monsoon flooding and drought every year in certain rotation. If the flood waters could be contained and used during periods of drought, the vast Indo Gangetic plane, where it never freezes, could grow three crops a year with modern farming practices.

Speaking of the monsoon season, I was the sole passenger on board a plane in Hyderabad one day where they had stopped to clean out the plane preparatory to leaving for New Delhi. I engaged a flight attendant in conversation. The young woman told me she had a lot of fun during monsoon standing up her dates in Bombay. She said that often the weather was such they could not land on a day when she had a date that evening. I then asked her if she was a Hindi in religion. She said she was. I inquired if it were not true that under her religion, she was not allowed to see, touch, or ever be alone with a man prior to marriage. She replied, "Those are old-fashioned ideas." European lifestyles were now circling the globe. In India, however, all marriages were still arranged by the parents. I asked a man one time how you stand being married to a woman selected by your parents, to which he replied, "The system works better than yours." Mohatma Gandhi once said, "In the West, you marry for love. In India, we learn to love the woman we marry."

One of the fallacies about India I learned in America was that women were regarded as inferior to men and that girl babies were often killed by throwing them in the Ganges River. I never saw one instance in India where women were not respected as much as men. Half the members of Parliament were women. A majority of physicians were women. There were as many girls as boys in school. India was the only major country in the world with a woman head of state.

The British acquired India as a source of raw materials to feed their industries. Indian leaders were educated in England, but the mass of the people were illiterate. There are many different languages and dialects spoken in India, but the British did three things that kept the country together after independence: 1. They established a system of courts and law based on the English judicial system where English was the means of communication. 2. They built, arguably, the best railroad system in the world. 3. The English language became the common denominator among the many languages.

My experiences in India convinced me of a number of things. American know-how, applied to India's basic problems, could create a wave of progress that could sweep all of Asia into a new century of progress. Also, I was convinced that the ultimate triumph of capitalism over communism would be determined whether or not it meets the human need for progress. I was convinced the outcome would never be determined by the Arms Race, the Cold War, or on any battlefield. The Communists won the war in Vietnam. Capitalism was winning in India, even with its limited vision, without firing a single shot.

I returned from India to my law practice in Omaha. Richard Nixon was elected President. Nebraska gave him the highest percentage of any state in the union and the war in Vietnam escalated. The cold, damp fog of failure settled over me.

After completing my mission in India and seeing my wife's race for Congress come to an end, I renewed my law practice. One day, my law partner, Frank B. Morrison, Jr. (Biff), came to me with news that would change his life and mine forever. He said he had found paradise and wanted to move there. I asked him where paradise was. He informed me it was Whitefish, Montana, a town at the head of the Flathead Valley in the northwest Rockies. He knew no one in

Montana but wanted to start a law practice in that small town in the mountains. To me, it sounded crazy at the time. However, my attempt to dissuade him failed. He moved. After Biff left, I withdrew from the firm and went into solo practice.

While in private practice, I was approached by a young man, a student at Creighton University and a citizen of Taiwan. He said that his government would like my wife, Maxine, and me to come to their country as guest of their government for a visit. They would pay all of our expenses, and there would be no obligations. Maxine and I boarded the Chinese airline at San Francisco and flew to Taipei. We were met by a talented young man who escorted us to the Grand Hotel, which is a magnificent place of exquisite Chinese architecture. We were scheduled for a series of social and political events. At no time was the controversy between the governments of Taiwan and the Communist government of mainland China mentioned. Our schedule included my giving a lecture at the Institute for International Relations at Taipei, and a train ride to the south for a visit to Gauchung, a free port into which raw materials could enter, be manufactured, and exported without tariff. The government would sell or rent factory space, the purpose being to provide employment for their citizens.

At a dinner in Taipei one night, the governor of Taiwan presented me with a beautiful painting of a Chinese harbor on a scroll. This is a valued memento of this enjoyable trip. Madam Chiang, who Maxine had met in Lincoln, was ill, but through her secretary presented Maxine with a group of her paintings.

Taiwan obviously enjoyed one of the world's most dynamic economies. I frequently thought that had Chiang Kai-shek governed mainland China as he governed Taiwan, there would never have been a Communist revolution. He was rid of the corruption and the military which characterized his mainland regime. He created a dynamic economy on Taiwan.

We returned to Omaha with a heightened interest in the future relationship between this highly capitalistic island and the vast Communist controlled mainland.

Just prior to my career as Public Defender in 1970, I became a candidate for the U.S. Senate for two reasons: I was becoming increasingly convinced that the war in Vietnam was a tragic mistake and I did not feel that our candidate, Dr. Wallace Peterson, head of the Department of Economics at the University of Nebraska was waging a vigorous enough campaign. I filed at the last minute and received the nomination. However, I was woefully lacking in campaign funds and was handicapped by the fact that many of my friends, not thinking I was available, had signed up with Peterson. I had two sources of help. My principal backer was the National Committee for a Livable World. Then, my son-in-law, Dr.

William Bennett Galloway, had completed his army service at Fort Jackson and returned to take over the campaign. I promised during the campaign that if President Nixon would send me to Vietnam and I did not secure a cease fire in a week, I would withdraw from the campaign. The offer was not accepted. The race was close enough. Walter Cronkite, longtime news anchor on CBS television, predicted my election, but it did not happen. Had I filed earlier and more clearly focused public attention on the fallacies of Vietnam and my experiences in India, I feel I could have been elected. Hindsight is always 20/20.

In 1970 the Board of County Commissioners offered me a challenging opportunity for public service by appointing me Public Defender. When I was appointed Douglas County Public Defender, I was impressed with the fact that "Equality Before the Law" is a motto, not a reality. A. Q. Wolfe had served for a number of years as Douglas County Public Defender. This office was the second oldest in the nation. Its only directive was to defend indigents charged with a felony who were unable to employ their own lawyer. A. Q., who had two or three assistant attorneys, was appointed Municipal Judge. Shortly after my appointment, the law mandated that the office add serious misdemeanors to the felony charge. This resulted in a greatly increased workload. I soon discovered that two factors prevented an adequate defense for our clients: 1. the excessive workload per lawyer, and 2. the lack of an investigator to discover facts and evidence.

It was impossible for ours, or any other public defender's office, to perform its duties adequately without knowing all of the facts of the case. An investigator with both training and experience is necessary to wade through the contentions and claims and find out what really happened. For the first time we hired an experienced retired detective from the police department. Our caseload, however, was so great it was impossible for him to do the job which needed to be done.

Another obstacle to the administration of justice was the lack of options available to the court in sentencing an offender. There was a great need for an adequate training and work program for nonviolent offenders. When I was Governor, one of the hurdles to putting prisoners to work was the opposition of organized labor to competition from so-called "criminals."

While I was serving as Public Defender, Congress had enacted the so-called Model Cities Act,[31] but this had only partially solved this problem. We brought a representative of the AFL-CIO, the leading labor union, into the office to become a joint probation officer with a Public Defender, thus, giving the court another tool to work with. For selected offenders, the court could place the offender on probation to the joint probation officers. The offender apprenticed to a skilled workman to learn a trade. This was a program which was in dire need of expansion.

I set out to find a competent black lawyer because half of our clients were black and I wanted to avoid the charge of discrimination. I built a staff of highly competent young lawyers. History justified my selection as most of them have become leaders in the Omaha Bar, one has been appointed U.S. District Judge, and another was elected to Congress. We were still unable to do an adequate job of representing thousands of clients.

One of the cases that landed in our office was the famous Rice-Poindexter murder case. Racial feelings in North Omaha were rampant. A radical organization of African-Americans known as the Black Panthers had created a group in North Omaha known as the Committee to Combat Fascism. A sixteen-year-old boy named Duane Peek had set a booby trap for the Omaha police which resulted in the death of a popular young policeman. Two militant young blacks named Rice and Poindexter were top officers in the Committee to Combat Fascism. Because of their hatred for the police and inflammatory rhetoric, the police and the FBI were lying in wait for them. When the police arrested Peek, he at first refused to implicate either Rice or Poindexter in the plot to kill a policeman, but after days of threats and promises of leniency, Peek contended that Rice and Poindexter had built the bomb and put him up to it.

Rice hired his own attorney and the court appointed the Public Defender to represent Poindexter. It was impossible for them to get a fair trial. They were largely convicted on the basis of Peek's testimony. Both received life sentences and became model prisoners. Poindexter completed his high school and college education and became an author while in prison.

Repeated attempts by local people and many all over America and abroad have pleaded with the Parole Board and the Pardon Board to grant a parole hearing, all to no avail. Thousands of people worldwide consider both of them to be political prisoners. I firmly believe that with adequate funds to investigate the case, we could have cleared both Rice and Poindexter in spite of the poisoned atmosphere created by racially inspired rhetoric.

I had been a prosecuting attorney, Governor, and Chairman of the Board of Pardons and Paroles. I was acquainted with many our justice system's shortcomings, but nothing brought it home to me like serving as Public Defender. In practice, there was no such thing as equality before the law. The need for a sentence review board was overwhelming. I have seen a judge put a man on probation for murder, then turn around and take a worker with a family to support off a job and give him forty years for an alleged forgery. I have seen a judge sentence a sixteen-year-old to death. Another judge promised leniency to a young man who insisted on his innocence after a jury found him guilty if he would admit his guilt. However, he promised to give him the maximum in prison if he failed to say he was guilty. This was duress of a virulent kind.

Guests at the home of Vice President Humphrey in Minnesota.

Society's refusal to mount an effective attack on the causes of crime or to correct obvious defects in our so-called correction system eventually led me to end my career as a public defender and return to private practice.

In 1974, I felt I could be more effective as Attorney General. My party nominated me, but I was defeated. I failed to convince the public why I should have the job, and a majority thought I was just seeking another way to stay on the public payroll. This was a tragic mistake of judgment on my part.

By 1972, I felt that the sacrifice of human life and material resources in Vietnam must be stopped. My friend, Senator George McGovern of South Dakota, became a candidate for President of the United States. I had first known him as head of the Food for Peace Program under President Kennedy and came to respect his idealism and ability. He would be a candidate against another friend, Vice President Hubert Humphrey, who had publicly supported President Johnson's prosecution of the war. McGovern asked me to be his campaign manager in Nebraska for the primary. Choosing one man over the other was one of the most difficult things I ever had to do. Humphrey had strongly supported me as Governor and had arranged for my assignment in India. This Nebraska campaign between Humphrey and McGovern could well determine the Democratic nominee for President.

Humphrey was a much closer friend than McGovern, but if democracy is to be meaningful, policy must prevail over friendship. This was a hard-fought campaign. McGovern won and went on to capture the Democratic nomination. I served as Chairman of the Nebraska delegation at the national convention.

My years of public service had prevented me from saving a sufficient nest egg for retirement. Our son, Biff, had become a successful trial lawyer in Montana. He influenced me to become his partner in buying Montana land on contract. By 1976, I was 71 years old and had no adequate savings. Biff convinced me to come to Montana and go into law practice with him because his wife, Sharon, was going to law school. He wanted me to come to Whitefish because he was opening an office in Missoula, the site of the state university.

---

30 Washington Post, Sept. 14, 1998. "Former Alabama Gov. George C. Wallace Dies," by
    Richard Pearson.

31 The Model Cities Act provided funds for programs to help solve some of the problems of the inner
    cities involving crime.

Life in Montana

I was admitted to the Montana Bar, bought an old home on beautiful Whitefish Lake, and started trying lawsuits all over western Montana. While we were there, Biff was elected to the Montana Supreme Court, served over six years, resigned to reenter private practice, and waged an unsuccessful campaign for governor.

While pursuing my legal career, I was making some money on the side with our land business, including the formation of two residential subdivisions.

As a trial lawyer in western Montana, I was associated with Dale McGarvey of Kalispell. I was also appointed to assist the Public Defender in Great Falls in defending a disbarred lawyer in Great Falls who had been charged with burglary. This resulted in a trial judge sustaining our motion for a directed verdict dismissing the case. During this period, I tried cases in Hamilton, Missoula, Boulder, Libby, Kalispell, Polson and Great Falls, as well as arguing a number of cases in the Montana Supreme Court.

Probably the most interesting case from a legal point of view was known as the Buffalo Block case in Kalispell. I represented some tenants whose offices had been destroyed when a large office building in which they were tenants burned. The fire started in a dental lab and spread throughout the building due to a violation of the fire and building codes adopted in a city ordinance by reference. This established new law in Montana which was that even though not spelled out in the ordinance, if adopted by reference, a violation thereof constituted negligence as a matter of law. The ordinance does not spell out the conditions for the code but refers to the code and adopts it by reference.

Montana was the site of a number of nuclear missile bases and a program was underway to establish a number of MX sites in Nebraska. The threat of nuclear confrontation consumed me. I became active in the Physicians for Social

Responsibility and the Nuclear Freeze Movement in Nebraska.

It was during this phase of my life as a trial lawyer in western Montana that I defended a young man named Nigel Cotier, charged in Federal Court with trespassing on a missile site near Great Falls. These missiles carried a nuclear warhead. He had a reasonable interpretation of the duty imposed upon him by the Declaration of Nuerenberg, which was made a part of federal law by Congress. This duty required citizens to protest actions by their government which constitute genocide and violate the laws of humanity. It could be said that the use of a nuclear weapon violated the ban on poison gas. Nigel climbed the fence at the nuclear site to enter an oral protest against it. He was arrested and charged with trespass. I volunteered to represent him pro bono. Judge Hatfield of the District Court found him guilty and gave him the maximum sentence, completely disregarding the law that motive, intention, and state of mind of the defendant are factors to consider in sentencing. I argued the case on appeal to the Ninth Circuit Court of Appeals but they affirmed the judgment. All of this convinced me that constitutional guarantees in this country mean nothing if the court perceives the act to violate what it perceives to be "national security."

The MX missiles being installed in western Nebraska were considered offensive nuclear weapons. I perceived this as making the civilian population of the area prime targets for a nuclear attack. This led to my giving speeches in the area voicing protest and contacting senators. Local support for the project was based on economic benefit to the area from government expenditures. I wondered how far are we willing to go to justify law violation for economic advantage.

During this period, I attempted to organize lawyers for social responsibility with no success. In addition, I authored a treatise called "A Magna Carta for the Nuclear Age."

After Biff's return to private practice in Whitefish, Maxine and I moved to Missoula and purchased a beautiful acre by Rattlesnake Creek. Our profits from the Northwoods Development, plus profit from the sale of our Whitefish home enabled us to build a winter home on a golf course in Sun Lakes, Arizona.

While Maxine and I were living in Missoula, Biff put together a delegation of lawyers to put on legal seminars in the USSR and the Peoples Republic of China. It was a fantastic educational opportunity. Among the things that surprised me in the Soviet Union was the extent to which they went to restore the trappings and buildings of the former royalty whom the Communists despised. A new profession was created called the restorationists. Their job was to restore buildings damaged in World War II to their original condition. In what is now called St.Petersburg and then in Moscow, we held seminars with lawyers, judges, and law professors. We compared our two legal systems. In Moscow we witnessed a trial. Certain selected members of our delegation met with members of the Supreme

Court of the Soviet Union. The trial was not much different from those in other European countries. They do not have juries. Two elected lay assessors sit with the law judge to hear the case. The case is then decided by a majority vote. We discovered that the criminal law and punishment for its violation did not differ much from our own. The great difference was a different treatment for "political crimes." They had separate courts to try those who threatened the state and the government.

In China, it was a different story. The country was just adopting capitalistic incentives, inviting foreign investors, and trying to recover from the Cultural Revolution. The Cultural Revolution was implemented by four dictators known as The Gang of Four. This Gang of Four and the so-called Cultural Revolution had tried to eradicate professionalism as we know it. They took professional people out of their offices and put them to physical work. Their court system was something totally alien to those of us who are heirs to the English system.

In this reawakening of China, we had the privilege of presenting to the University of Peking its first set of American law books: Am.Jur 2nd, meaning the second edition of *American Jurisprudence*.

Probably my greatest surprise in China was our visit to the Municipal Penitentiary of Shanghai. It made more sense than any prison I have seen anywhere. The woman warden escorted us on our tour. She used good English and was obviously well trained. There was no idleness. Except for the cells, it resembled a factory more than a prison. Prisoners attended class four hours a day. Those with music or artistic talent were trained in their skill. One floor was devoted to prisoners working on machines making watch cases. After serving their time or being paroled, they were put to work at the same job for which they were trained in prison. Recidivism was almost nonexistent. The penitentiary cost the city or state nothing; it made a profit. I thought there was a real lesson to be learned here.

In Beijing, we were quartered in the beautiful official houses where Henry Kissinger and the American delegation stayed during the opening of relations between our two countries. In Beijing, I met a man born the same day I was who was still practicing law. He had lived in China under the Monarchy, the Republic, the Chiang Kai-shek regimes, the Communist Revolution, Mao Tsi Tung, the Cultural Revolution, and modern China. What an experience!

We stopped in Tokyo on our return for a conference with Ambassador Mike Mansfield. At dinner in Tokyo, I was struck with an abdominal pain which required a gallbladder operation by the time we hit Helena, Montana.

Trying jury cases is strenuous business. As I approached my eightieth birthday, moving to a new retirement community in Sun Lakes, Arizona seemed attractive. We sold our home on the Rattlesnake in Missoula and decided to spend more time in Arizona. This was a mistake. Approaching my eightieth birthday, I wanted to retire from trying jury cases but not retire from life. In Arizona, I tried commuting from Sun Lakes to Phoenix to do research for a law firm, including work in the Arizona State University Law Library. This commuting in heavy traffic was too much for an old man. I loved our home and the yard work, but I was not ready to spend the rest of my life playing golf, pool, shuffleboard, cards, and drinking at the club.

Our life in Sun Lakes was something most people can only dream about. Our front yard was typical Arizona: Visqueen covered with gravel, and two palm trees. We had the back yard surrounded with cement block painted white with the exception of the back which was enclosed with black iron grill see through which faced the golf course. My back yard was planted to grass and had automatic sprinklers. In this part of the yard I planted one grapefruit, one lemon, and two orange trees which produced a great volume of citrus. Opposite the kitchen we had a pass through window onto a patio which I called my playpen. Here I frequently barbequed our meat. Only one side of the patio was open. The west side was the outside east wall of our bedroom. It contained a cabinet and the most beautiful climbing rose I have ever seen. Our area was known as Phase One of the Sun Lakes Country Club. We had a beautiful clubhouse which contained a restaurant, a dance floor, library, pool room, shuffleboard court, tennis courts, indoor and outdoor swimming pools, and a gymnasium. The developer aided in the construction of a church close to the schoolhouse where a non-denominational fundamentalist preacher painted a picture of a hereafter even more beautiful than the Sun Lakes Country Club. This heaven was paved with golden streets and was completely divorced from the troubles of the world. The price of admission was to accept Christ as your personal Savior and not be bothered with the world's hungry diseased children, the nuclear arms race which threatened human existence on the planet, or other problems that plagued humanity on this earth. This church was later converted to a United Church of Christ where my wife became a moderator. They hired an able retired preacher who was concerned with the world's problems and, therefore, offended some of the congregation.

My guilty conscience at not contributing to the solution of this world's problems weighed heavily on me. This condition was helped some by becoming active as an honorary member of the Physicians for Social Responsibility, whose chief aim was to end civilization's march to nuclear annihilation. A public meeting sponsored by nationally prominent physicians was held at Arizona State University. Out of the forty thousand plus students on the campus, probably twenty-five students were interested enough to show up, while hundreds paid an admission fee with standing room only to hear one of the Watergate convicts lecture on how to corrupt the political process. I have never fully recovered from this disappointment at one of America's great universities. This was no doubt a factor in my eventual return to Nebraska and reality.

One of the family disappointments during our stay in Arizona was the divorce of daughter-in-law Jerry and our son David Jon. They had two precious young children. While I was practicing law in Omaha after my governorship, David Jon quit the construction business in Beaumont, Texas and came to Omaha with his wife and two children. After a number of real estate deals and building a shopping center in Fremont, he decided to join Jerry's relatives in the construction business in Pensacola, Florida. This did not work out and Jerry and David became estranged. After an almost complete emotional collapse, he came to live with us in Arizona. During this time, he worked for a while in Polson, Montana and built a house in Sun Lakes. Then he went into the house construction business in Casa Grande, Arizona. This was quite successful. He sold motor homes, took painting lessons and became quite a good artist. He met a young widow, Sandra Juster, and they became live-in partners. She was an experienced sales lady and department manager at J. C. Penney's. I assisted them in buying a home in Chandler. After we moved back up to Lincoln, she was transferred to Las Vegas, Nevada where they now live.

Our friend, Larry Price, the hamburger king of Lincoln, for whom my wife had served as public relations director when he took King's public, had become one of Lincoln's prime real estate developers. He purchased the Stuart Building, an important office building in downtown Lincoln. Many offices were moving out to the suburbs so Larry converted the building into condominiums.

For years, he and his employee, Bill Kerrey, brother of U.S. Senator Bob Kerrey, had attempted to sell us a condo. We rejected the idea, but Larry continued to hold space for us. After about five years of persuading, Larry offered to build a condo to our specifications and trade it for our home at Sun Lakes. In 1990, we closed the deal and moved to Lincoln.

I wanted to become active at something worthwhile. I felt that I had a lot of unfinished business in the area of public policy. I was friendly with Republican Governor Kay Orr whose husband, Bill, had been a neighbor of my niece and her husband in Columbus Junction, Iowa.

On the Democratic side, the field was crowded with friends. Former Governor Bob Kerrey was in the U.S. Senate. Bill Harris, the Mayor of Lincoln, grew up with our kids; his parents were among our closest friends. Ben Nelson, who my wife had taught in kindergarten; former Mayor of Omaha Mike Boyle who our son Biff had promoted as president of the young Democrats; and Dr. Prokoff were all friends.

The Criminal Justice System

After Ben Nelson took office as governor, I went to his office to register my concerns about the criminal justice system. Sandra Scofield, his Chief of Staff, handed me a thick file and told me to go to work on it because she did not have time. I had a new, fascinating, full-time job without pay. I interviewed teachers, corrections officials, judges, and law enforcers and read articles on the subject, all of which were added to my previous experience in the field.

I made certain recommendations to the Governor. Former Governor Kay Orr had appointed a Task Force on prison overcrowding and alternatives to incarceration. Many studies had been made. I thought we needed action rather than another study. The present Governor thought otherwise and appointed me co-chairman of a task force on the same subject.

We plowed the same old ground. Crime prevention was beyond our mandate, but was critically important to reduced incarceration. A governor cannot reform human character but he can serve as a catalyst to bring students, teachers, correction officials, prosecutors, judges, probation and parole people together to work out a program for youth which will bring them into the system rather than make them become antagonistic to it. I came to the conclusion that prisons should be to retrain dangerous people or those who refuse rehabilitation. Even for those incarcerated, we were badly in need of work and educational programs to prepare prisoners to live outside in the event of release, thereby greatly reducing recidivism.

Those who advocate policies which depart from accepted practices at the time encounter great resistance and criticism. Most effective steps for social progress are filtered through this environment.

My years as prosecuting attorney, public defender, Governor, Chairman of the Board of Pardons and Paroles, parent, teacher, school administrator and trial lawyer convinced me that capital punishment was barbaric, unnecessary, and irrational because: 1. I felt it was not effective and increased and did not decrease violence. 2. I did not think any human being or human institution had the ability to determine who should live and who should die. I was opposed to the state getting into the murder business. 3. It consumed vast resources needed to attack the causes of crime. 4. There was the danger of executing innocent people and application of the death penalty was highly discriminatory. 5. I felt murderers should be imprisoned, put to work and made to use their earnings in prison to attack the causes of crime and support the dependents of those they killed, if any.

I felt that all non-violent prisoners should be removed from prison with violent offenders and be put to work in community correction programs. I thought that all prisoners should be required to attend class and work. I felt the state should coordinate the efforts of fragmented agencies dealing with crime and inspire an all-out citizens' effort to attack the causes of crime before it happens. Being unsuccessful in convincing the Legislature and the Governor to adopt my recommendations, I decided to start programs over which I had more control.

The Great Platte River Road
Archway Monument

For six years I had officed in a building which had a number of admonitions carved in stone. Among them were these: "The salvation of the state is the watchfulness in the citizen." "Political society exists for the sake of Noble Living."[32] In many ways I was seeing irresponsibility replace responsibility as a human characteristic. I had seen a trend of disrespect and disinterest in the political process. I had seen growing disinterest in history, where we had come from and where we were going. In my own state of Nebraska events occurred which helped convert a nation into a vast continental empire on whose leadership and example the future of mankind depends. I became concerned that increasing numbers of people were not interested in their heritage.

I became increasingly aware of the necessity to build a monument depicting the evolution of communication and transportation which led to the creation of a vast continental empire, one global community, and the advent of man's moving into outer space. I also became convinced of the necessity to memorialize the evolution of communication, which helped create the global community, discovering truth, and possibly leading eventually to inter-global communication.

One of my convictions was that the invention of the wheel, human language, and the printing press, with its twin sisters of radio and television, had changed human life on this planet forever. Human mobility and the transfer of information were the foundation of civilization.

I had located and led the team which built I-80 over the "Great Platte River Road" in central Nebraska. It had become the most heavily traveled transcontinental highway in America and generally followed the historic route of the Great Platte River Road. In excess of twelve thousand travelers a year used this highway without the slightest idea of the historical importance of the route.

I am a great believer in the old Chinese proverb that any civilization which is unmindful of its past is like a tree cut off from its roots or a brook cut off from its water source. I feel that the Great Platte River Road is one of the most historic places on earth. It was here that the Oregon, California, and Mormon Trails converged and moved west to convert a nation into a vast continental empire. It was here that we witnessed the wagon trails give way to the first transcontinental highway. It was here that the Indian smoke signals gave way to the Pony Express, then to the first transcontinental telephone and telegraph lines, the first transcontinental railroad which bound the continent together, then the first transcontinental airline. Then followed I-80 and the first transcontinental fiberoptic cable. This was the only place on earth where all of these things occurred. It should be memorialized.

I went to my old friend, J. Gregg Smith, with my idea. He thought it was a great idea and said it should take the form of an archway over I-80. We went to Governor Nelson. He endorsed the idea enthusiastically and said he would look for some money to implement it. Some weeks later, he told us the highway department would cooperate, but he could not find any money to build it. After the *Omaha World-Herald* published a story about my idea, I was approached by Ron Tillery who introduced himself as Director of Economic Development for Buffalo County. He told me that the city of Kearney was interested in the idea. He approached the motel industry who wanted to furnish money to hire experts to plan the memorial. The city council authorized the industry to levy a small tax on the guest bill to fund it. We formed a nonprofit corporation to build and operate the memorial. The original board of directors consisted of Peter Katsiopolis, Mayor of Kearney; James Leuschen, Omaha businessman and civic leader; and Frank B. Morrison, Sr.

Gregg Smith set about contacting former Disney people. We hired an architectural firm, Urban Design, from Denver; some former Disney people from Orlando; Dayton Duncan of New Hampshire as Historian; a Cambridge, Massachusetts firm as creator of the program; and Peter Kiewit of Omaha as builder. Pete Peterson, a former Kearney boy, recommended that we approach Soloman Smith Barney for financing. This resulted in the City of Kearney issuing revenue bonds that were sold by Smith Barney, and we started construction of the Great Plains River Road Memorial

The idea of using Disney methodology and modern technology to bring authentic history alive and to make their heritage more real and relevant was a relatively new idea. When the news story first broke that we intended to build a structure whose original design was printed therein unleashed a storm of protests. Unmindful of the gripping story to be told inside the structure, the Dean of Architecture at the University of Nebraska openly attacked the design. When asked to meet with our architect to alter the design, he said he opposed the whole project and persuaded the State Society of Architects to oppose it. Chris Beutler, one of the ablest and most respected members of the Legislature organized opposition to the design.

A Lincoln man, Bob Van Valkinburgh, went to Kearney and organized some land owners in the area to oppose the project and went so far as to threaten to impeach the mayor. Construction of what became known in the state as the Archway Project became the most controversial subject of discussion. Most people did not understand it and did not think it would ever be built. We employed a well known national artist from Yale University to design the controversial icons on top of the Archway but controversy continued. A structure of this nature had never been built over an interstate highway anywhere in the United States. We were confronted with countless environmental, safety, highway, traffic, signage, and a host of other regulations. We had much publicity in the media over the controversy but little editorial support. *Newsweek* magazine made a joke of the project and the argument over design. One nationally prominent newspaper compared our project to a proposed spike in the railroad yard in North Platte and a pile of baled hay in Kansas.

We organized a statewide Educational Advisory Committee, had the full support of the State Highway Department and the University of Nebraska at Kearney. The Chamber of Commerce and the City Council of Kearney were steadfast in their support all through the controversy. An organization is now created to bring school children from all over America to visit the Archway.

Through all of these difficulties, the Archway emerged. It was built beside the road and rolled over the highway one night. It is the largest object ever to have been rolled over a highway in the history of Nebraska and the only historic monument ever to bridge an interstate highway.

When Jim Leuschen was killed in an automobile accident, Joe McCartney of Omaha took his place. Ron Tillery, Ron Larson, Jim Exon, and John Mitchell were added to the board of directors.

It is my ambition that this Great Platte River Road Memorial which spans Interstate 80 will be a catalyst around which will develop a vast new educational and research program. The University of Nebraska at Kearney should become the force behind this curriculum. This program must include research into the cultural, economic, social, and political impact of the evolution of transportation and communication. It must suggest how to deal with it. Rapid transportation and instant communication are making the entire world one community and bringing the cosmos closer and closer to our consciousness. Human ability to comprehend and deal with this new reality is essential to human progress and perhaps even survival.

We were delayed in construction and did not open to the public until June 9,

2000. Our Board of Directors, their employees and the Chancellor of the University of Nebraska at Kearney immediately thereafter started a program to convince President Clinton of the educational and cultural importance of the Archway and the role of the University of Nebraska at Kearney. Many letters and telephone calls were sent to him and his staff. The President became convinced of the historical importance of the project. We were notified that he would arrive in Kearney on December 8, 2000 to visit the Archway and deliver a major policy address at the University of Nebraska at Kearney. In his address at the University he stressed the fact that we were now one global community interdependent economically and culturally. This carried out the theme of the Archway Monument that the evolution of transportation and instant communication had produced this result.

As former U. S. Senator and Governor J. J. Exon, our Assistant Manager Ronnie Obrien and I escorted the President through the Archway, I explained to him that the last two stages of human mobility, the airplane and space age, were planned but not yet added to our story of the evolution of transportation and communication. I was happy and pleased that the President of the United States approved and complimented our project, including the plaque of dedication.

The human urge to travel and communicate is now reaching into outer space. For me, the final experience of travelers through the Archway must be a simulated travel in a spaceship into the cosmos.

The air age and the space age are now in their infancy. The future staggers our imagination. To achieve progress in this area demands leadership on the part of our presidents. John Kennedy was dedicated to extraterrestrial travel and became the father of the American space age, which was then so ably carried on by President Johnson.

My readers should know something about my relationships with these two presidents I worked with so closely as governor. I shall relate some of my experiences with them outside of their interest in the space age.

32 These quotations are carved into the stone on the Nebraska State Capitol building and were chosen for placement there by Hartley Burr Alexander, the architect.

Then President of the United States, Bill Clinton, recognized the historical importance of the Arch with his official visit. After praising and dedicating the Arch, he requested that I autograph his pre-publication copy of my book, "My Journey Through the Twentieth Century". Senator J. James Exon looks on.

John F. Kennedy

John Kennedy was elected President of the United States on the same day I was elected Governor of the State of Nebraska. A few days after I assumed the responsibility of the Nebraska governorship, Maxine and I flew to Washington to attend the inauguration of John Kennedy as President and Lyndon B. Johnson as Vice-President of the United States. Upon arrival there, we found one of the most bitterly cold and disagreeable days you can imagine. The snow was deep and people unaccustomed in that part of the United States to driving in snow found themselves in traffic jams all over town.

The inaugural committee had built a platform on the east side of the Capitol building. Fifty governors, the Chief Justice of the United States, members of Congress, and those involved in the ceremony sat on the snow-covered platform facing a biting wind. We observed Robert Frost, one of the President-elect's favorite poets, rise to deliver one of his favorite poems. The wind was so strong it blew some of the papers away and he was forced to improvise. We heard the Cardinal deliver his lengthy prayer and the Chief Justice of the United States administer the oath of office to this young man who was to assume the most awesome responsibility in human history. This was the office which Adlai Stephenson had described as having such potential for good or evil that it staggered the imagination and converted arrogance to prayer.

Then followed the speech that made the agony of the bone-chilling afternoon worthwhile. The acceptance speech of the first President of the United States born in the twentieth century gave America a new challenge and new vision of where we were and the direction in which we should go. He emphasized the long pull ahead and stated that during this era, we should ask not what our government can do for us but what we can do for our country. He closed by saying that here on earth, "God's work must truly be our own." Many, many times since that day, I have wondered just what God's work is that we are to do on this planet.

After the inauguration, we were assigned limousines, and passed the long, long inaugural parade, while the President of the United States stood in review with all the agony imposed by this disagreeable day. That night was the inaugural ball. America had a new President and a new Vice-President, and all of us were looking forward to exciting days ahead.

The next few years brought many happy associations with the new President. Not long after his inauguration, Maxine and I received an invitation to attend a state dinner at the White House. Neither one of us had ever been inside the White House before. We reported for the pre-dinner ceremonies, which were attended by high profile people from all over America - politicians, leaders of industry, Hollywood moguls, entertainers, and other figures. Jackie Kennedy had put her classic stamp on everything that went on in the White House.

After dinner, we adjourned for entertainment, the character of which is seldom heard at official functions. Entertainment consisted of Basil Rathbone reading Elizabethan poetry to string music accompaniment. In front of us sat the new first lady of America, accompanied by Lyndon B. Johnson, the new Vice-President. He was the product of the rugged, uncouth country of southwest Texas.

After this event, there were many times that I had occasion to visit Washington on official business with Orville Freeman, the outstanding Secretary of Agriculture. Freeman had been Governor of Minnesota. He had graduated Phi Beta Kappa from the University of Minnesota and played football there. He was a man with a photographic memory and a sharp mind.

Secretary of the Interior, Stuart Udahl, was also a man with whom we were to have many contacts. Stuart Udall was a product of America's great Southwest. As Secretary of the Interior, he was dedicated to preserving our environment. His brother Morris was a longtime Congressman from Tucson, Arizona, whose campaign for the Presidency I managed in the Nebraska primary until he withdrew in favor of Senator Frank Church, whose successful Nebraska primary was managed by my wife Maxine.

The President himself was available anytime I was in Washington and had important business to transact. I remember on one occasion, I called the White House without a formal appointment. Kenny O'Donnell, one of the so-called Irish Mafia of Boston, an old friend of the President, was appointment secretary and he wasn't going to let me in. The President's private secretary was Evelyn Lincoln, a Nebraska woman and friend of mine. She saw me in O'Donnell's office and motioned for me to come forward and follow her. Then she ushered me in the side door of the oval office so I could visit with the President.

In 1962, it was my desire to take over the job of Chief Justice of the Nebraska Supreme Court. I was a lawyer who loved the law and thought I would enjoy the office of the Chief Justice. I was acquiring ideas which I thought would be improvements in the judicial process.

In those days, judges were elected, and I could have had the job almost by acclamation because no other Nebraskan would have the opportunity for publicity and recognition that the governor would have during the campaign.

Before making up my mind, I decided to pay a visit to the President of the United States and tell him what I had in mind. I thought I owed him this obligation because of his interest and the support that he had given me in my race for the United States Senate and the governorship of Nebraska. I went to Washington and conferred with the President. He was adamant that he wanted me to be a part of his team. He said he would do anything within his power to be helpful during the campaign.

He sent me over to see John Bailey, then Chairman of the Democratic National Committee, who offered me full control over all patronage in the state of Nebraska. I told him that this was a headache that I did not want. However, I did not want it placed in the hands of anybody who would use it to build a personal political power base that would interfere with the administration of state government or putting the best people in charge of policy implementation.

I arrived at an agreement with Bailey. Political patronage in the state of Nebraska would be placed in the hands of Maureen Biegert, the Democratic National Committeewoman. I felt she would never use it for personal power or in any way inhibit my administration. Bailey agreed to this and said he would be helpful in any way he could.

At that time Kennedy was not only an American leader, he was a world leader in a period of critical decisions. Any nation which owned a weapon so powerful that it had the potential to destroy human life on this planet was so awesome that I felt I should remain in political office. This was a world leader who would send a man to the moon and lead our nation into outer space.

I left Washington with a determination that I was going to contest the governorship and campaign on my record of the first two years.

The Republicans, as predicted, nominated my friend, Fred Seaton. My relationships with the White House continued to be close and cordial. During the 1962 campaign, somebody had apparently tipped Seaton off to the fact that my relationship with the Kennedys had been close. He seized upon that as a campaign issue. He asserted that Nebraska's state government was being operated in Washington, and that decisions with reference to the operation of state government of Nebraska were coming out of the White House. I telephoned him and said, "Fred, you know this isn't true. Why are you saying it?" All he said was, "I'm going to keep on saying it from now until election."

One night, I was speaking at a Democratic banquet and the thought came to me as to how to handle this situation. During the course of my talk, I pointed out that the President of the United States had the most awesome responsibility in human history. He lived with problems all over the world, twenty-four hours a day, and was never divorced from having his mind occupied with this awesome responsibility. At that time there was a problem in central Africa and the African Congo. There were also trouble spots worldwide.

I said the way the President and I handled this was as follows: every morning before he went into a conference with the Secretary of State or into a cabinet meeting, he called me on the phone and said, "Frank, this is Jack. How are we getting along with that road up south of Stanton, Nebraska?"

The whole thing was a farce and a non-issue. In fact, before his assassination, I was talking to him on the telephone from my office in the statehouse in Lincoln. It was on that occasion the President asked me how I was getting along with the road up south of Stanton, Nebraska.

In 1963, we were having the annual Midwest Governors' Conference in Omaha, over which I was presiding as chairman. We adjourned that noon and were prepared to visit the Strategic Air Command south of Omaha. The bombers there were prepared to release nuclear bombs in a quantity which had the potential to end human life on this planet.

That noon before leaving for the office, I encountered a young man in the lobby of the Fontenelle Hotel by the name of Fletcher Knebel. He was co-author of *Seven Days in May*, a fictional story of a successful military coup that took over the government of the United States. I have often thought about this coincidence.

Governor Romney of Michigan, my vice-chairman, and I boarded a bus and went south for our visit to the Strategic Air Command. We drove up in front of the administration building, left the bus, and I noticed General Power. As we approached, he called me to one side and notified me personally that he thought the President of the United States had been assassinated. I was stunned. Chilling thoughts ran through my mind, particularly since I had just visited with Fletcher Knebel. We went on into the administration building where General Power had set up television screens and we watched the proceedings in the hospital in Dallas until the President was pronounced dead. None of us knew the full significance of this assassination. We returned immediately to the hotel. I called the governors into session and discussed our next step. Unanimously, they voted to adjourn immediately and return home where they would ask the public to call off all major meetings of any size to avoid any terrorism or disruption.

I returned to Lincoln immediately. This was the day before the annual Oklahoma-Nebraska football game, which always was a sellout with an enormous crowd. I called Coach Bob Devaney and notified him of our action. He said it was all right with him to postpone or call off the game if it was agreeable to Coach Bud Wilkenson, who was then physical fitness director under Kennedy for the United States and football coach of the University of Oklahoma. I notified Wilkenson of our action and my conversation with Devaney. He had all kinds of excuses as to why he could neither continue nor cancel the game. I have always wondered how Coach Wilkenson could be this unconcerned about the public safety of the United States, but in any event, I returned home, called Devaney and told him of my conversation with Wilkenson. I notified Devaney that I was leaving for Washington the next day for the President's funeral, and I wanted to leave one message with him. "Tell the Nebraska football team to demonstrate for Coach Wilkenson exactly what a group of physically fit young men could do." That is exactly what the Nebraska team did the next day.

The following morning, after our arrival in Washington, Maxine and I were invited to come to the White House to pay our respects. We entered the north door of the White House and the first person to greet us was the Attorney General of the United States, the brother of the assassinated President, who had been up all night greeting people. This was a Bobby Kennedy I had never known before. Here was the tough, cocky, political operative who had managed the Kennedy campaign. Here was the tough law enforcing officer of the United States who had defied rebellion, who had defied the governor of Alabama who stood at the gate at the University of Alabama to deny admission to any African-American. Here was the man who defied the governor and ushered the black students in the back door of the school building at the University of Alabama.

The Bobby we saw the day of the funeral was a man who was humble, physically shaken, and whose eyes were puffy and glazed. What devotion! What dedication to his country, his brother and to his responsibility! This was a change in Robert Kennedy that continued up to the time of his own assassination.

After we paid our respects at the White House, we were assigned places in the funeral parade and went to the cathedral for the religious service. Probably never before in all of human history had so many heads of state, so many representatives of governments all over the world gathered together in one church to pay their respects to a fallen leader of a government and to pay homage to that entity which is the merciful father of us all. I noticed to my side in another pew was General DeGaule, the dictator of France, on his knees in humble prayer. Behind him and to his left was the husband of the Queen of England. In front of us and to our left was former Vice-President Richard Nixon, who had been Senator Kennedy's opponent in the presidential election.

The thought occurred to me: Why cannot we, the passengers of this little spaceship we call the Earth, come together in harmony and unity and respect in times of prosperity and peace like we do on this occasion of international tragedy?

After the church service, we assembled in assigned limousines. Astronaut John Glenn, our original traveler into outer space, and his wife rode with Maxine and me. That was the first time I had ever met personally with Senator Glenn. It was a sad and quiet trip to Arlington Cemetery where we passed by the grave and paid our respects to the man who had given this nation a new vision of its potential and who had excited people all over the world as to what we could be. Thus came to an end the leadership of John F. Kennedy. He was dead, but his impact upon this country and the world would never be forgotten. The father of America's venture into outer space had passed into history and the torch was passed to his successor, Lyndon B. Johnson.

Lyndon B. Johnson

On the afternoon of President Kennedy's funeral, the new leader of our country sent a notice to all of the governors of the United States that he wanted to meet with them at his office in the Executive Building. All but Texas Governor John Connally, who was hospitalized in Dallas, assembled. It must have been at least 10:00 p.m. when Johnson walked in. He first announced that the worst problem the world faced was the problem of hate. He did not offer a solution to this serious disease, but he did give us a challenge in these words: "We have lost our leader. He had an agenda for this nation. It is our responsibility to see that agenda is carried out. I cannot do it alone, but with your help and God's help, we can." The weeks that followed were some of the most productive in our nation's history.

Lyndon B. Johnson was probably the most complex, and one of the most interesting, people it has been my pleasure to know. I first met the majority leader of the United States Senate in Omaha in the spring of 1960 at the home of Bernard J. Boyle.

Bernard J. "Bernie" Boyle, was an impressive, imposing Omaha lawyer of Irish descent who had a magnificent home on Hickory Street on what was then the western edge of Omaha. He had an expansive bluegrass backyard that sloped to the south of his home where he frequently held receptions for distinguished political guests.

One of the helpful things that Bernie did was to invite delegates, or candidates for delegates to the Democratic National Convention to meet candidates for the presidency. Although Bernie and I were both pledged to support Senator John F. Kennedy at the upcoming Democratic National Convention, he afforded the opportunity for us to meet other presidential candidates. Among these was Lyndon B. Johnson, a United States Senator from Texas who was then majority leader of the United States Senate.

Senator Johnson was accompanied by a number of people, including a man named Baker who was an influence peddler of some note. Also with him was an outstanding, and later famous, assistant, John Connally. This interesting meeting lasted most of the afternoon.

My next visit, one on one, with my future friend, was when he was Vice-President of the United States in the year 1963 while I was attending the annual Governors' Conference in Miami, Florida. When I was hit by an infection caused by a prostate operation, I was confined to my hotel bed, and Johnson came to call.

One of the more interesting sessions I ever had with President Johnson was in the election of 1964. I received a call from the White House at my office, the governor's office in Lincoln, Nebraska. It notified me that the president was flying in to Offutt Air Force Base, south of Omaha, and he would like a meeting that afternoon with one of the largest contractors and builders in the world, Peter Kiewit of Kiewit Construction Company. I was asked to contact Mr. Kiewit and have him there. I replied that I could come, but Mr. Kiewit was a leading American executive who traveled all over the world. I had no idea whether, on that short notice, I'd be able to find him and have him there, but I promised to try.

Immediately, I called Kiewit at his office and, as luck would have it, he was there. I told him about my call from the White House. Of course, when one is doing billions of dollars of business with the federal government, and the President asks to meet with you, you have a tendency to obey.

We were there only a short time and in came Air Force One. The Commanding General and his troops went out to escort the Commander in Chief from Air Force One into the Commanding General's office at SAC. The Strategic Air Command, as we all know, was charged with the defense of the North American continent. The bombers were equipped with nuclear weapons. It was probably the most destructive force ever assembled by any nation in human history. General Power escorted the President to his office in the command headquarters. Kiewit and I followed along. General Power ushered the Commander in Chief into his office. After we entered, he closed the door and left.

In that office was the President of the United States, his Chief of Staff, Peter Kiewit, and myself. I was conscious that the President of the United States had power with modern technology that our forebears would have thought unbelievable. By issuing an order, he could have extinguished all human life on this planet. What an awesome responsibility to be conferred by a people on any single human being.

It was in the awesomeness of the office of the Commanding General of the Strategic Air Command and in the presence of the Commander in Chief of the Armed Forces of the United States and Chief Executive of this nation that Lyndon B. Johnson, President of the United States, looked at Peter Kiewit and me and

A conference with the President in the Oval Office.

reeled off a number of reasons why he wished to be elected President of the United States in his own right. He had acquired that office by virtue of the tragedy of the assassination of President Kennedy, but he outlined why he desired to be elected President of the United States. He was going to depend upon Kiewit and me to carry the state of Nebraska for him in the upcoming election. The President told Kiewit it was not good for his or anybody's business to have four changes of administration in four years.

Peter Kiewit owned the *Omaha World-Herald*, which was by far the most powerful and most read newspaper in the state of Nebraska. In addition, he owned Channel 7, the ABC outlet in Omaha. The *Omaha World-Herald* was one of the strongest Goldwater supporters in the United States and had been very critical of the Johnson administration. After President Johnson issued his mandate to Peter Kiewit and me, there was a lull in the conversation for a minute. I spoke up and said, "Mr. President, I plan on supporting you, but I can't speak for Mr. Kiewit." Whereupon, Mr. Kiewit told the President that he had absolutely nothing to do with the editorial policy of the newspaper, and that his relationship with the newspaper was only that of an owner. Never on any occasion did he interfere with the editorial policy of the newspaper. Then he said he would be glad to speak with the boys, meaning the boys responsible for the editorial policy of the newspaper at that time. After fifteen minutes or so of this conversation, the conference ended, the Commander in Chief of the Armed Forces of the United States, the President, the most powerful man in human history, went back to Washington. Mr. Kiewit and I returned to our respective offices.

Peter Kiewit was never active in politics. I always assumed he was a silent Republican. I am sure Johnson convinced him that four changes of administration in four years was not good for his business or anyone's business. The only thing he ever said to me after this encounter was that he liked Johnson and that his head was screwed on right. The *World-Herald* and Channel 7 could not in good conscience switch to Johnson, but after the Kiewit meeting they changed to neutral.

One day, I was presiding over a meeting of the Board of Pardons and Paroles, when Lady Bird Johnson, First Lady of the United States, called to invite Maxine and me to Washington. We were to be overnight guests of the President and Mrs. Johnson, attend a state dinner, and enjoy a rendition of *Oklahoma* by a professional cast in the Rose Garden the following morning. The Rose Garden is that area immediately south of the White House. A special large covered platform was built there on which the original cast of *Oklahoma* performed. The cast was reduced in size, but our friend Gordon McRae, who was married to a Nebraska girl, was with the cast. He had played the hero Curley both on Broadway and in the movie version.

Although we had been guests of the White House on other occasions, Maxine and I had never spent a night at the White House. We had a most enjoyable evening. As we attended the rendition of *Oklahoma* in the Rose Garden at the White House, I thought this was quite a contrasting style of entertainment to the last state dinner we attended at the White House when President Kennedy and Jackie were there and the entertainment had consisted of Elizabethan poetry put to string music.

In any event, this gave us an opportunity to feel quite at home in the White House, the home of the President of the United States and the scene of many historical decisions which influenced not only our lives but the lives of people all over the world.

With reference to the Vietnam War, all of the United States governors were asked to attend a one time briefing at the White House in order to hear the justification of the war and what our goals were. The President sent Air Force One out to pick up a group of governors for the conference.

At our briefing session in Washington, the case for the Vietnam War was presented by Secretary MacNamara, Dean Rusk, the Secretary of State, the Chairman of the Joint Chiefs, the President of the United States, and so forth. In retrospect, I look back on these briefings and it is hard to believe that these brilliant men had access to information that the rest of the nation didn't, that they were the beneficiaries of the lessons of history, and that they could be motivated in the prosecution of this war by fallacies and a misinterpretation of history and for objectives that history has proved to be false and invalid.

One day in the fall of 1966, I was notified by the White House that the President was flying into Omaha to conduct a ceremony with reference to the shipments of wheat on the Missouri River destined for India as an historical benchmark. This was during the campaign, and we gathered on the banks of the Missouri River with the President and a full array. Among those present were my son, Frank, Jr.; his law partner, Don Lay, a famous trial lawyer in Omaha; and United States District Attorney in Omaha, Ted Richling, both of whom wanted an appointment to the United States 8th Circuit Court of Appeals.

My son's law partner had never met the President. Biff brought him over and asked me to introduce him to the President, which I did. After the ceremony was over, the President asked me if I would accompany him on Air Force One on his flight to Des Monies where he was to give a talk that evening. On the airplane was his youngest daughter's future husband and the ever-present secret service. Johnson was in the process of changing clothes in the bathroom when he asked me to come back. He wanted to have an intimate visit with me. The visit was about the appointment to the 8th Circuit Court of Appeals. He asked me about this man, Don Lay, and his background. The Justice Department was aware of the fact that the other candidates, such as Judge Hale McCowan of the Nebraska Supreme Court was a Democrat, but McCowan had been a friend and classmate of Richard Nixon at Duke University Law School and had ended up in a Democrats for Nixon organization. Burt Overcash, a highly able lawyer who was a friend of mine and personal counsel to me as Governor, had a law partner by the name of Smith. Smith was Carl Curtis' campaign manager for the United States Senate and had given press releases very uncomplimentary about the Johnson administration and my administration which didn't help Burt's cause any.

I am sure all of these candidates knew that the appointment was mine for the asking. Johnson gave me the impression that if I did not accept the nomination, it was going to Lay. In consenting to run for the Senate, Johnson had promised me the appointment to the Court if I lost. This kid from Wildcat Creek was riding on Air Force One, the most prestigious airplane in the world, locked in a bathroom conference with the most powerful man in the world. As a lawyer I had informed President Kennedy I wanted to be Chief Justice of the Nebraska Supreme Court. I had, prior to my filing for the Senate, notified Johnson of my desire to be appointed to the vacancy on the U. S. Circuit Court of Appeals. Here I was face to face with the man who had the power to change history. I had an opportunity to take a job which would not only insure my lifetime financial security, but give me an opportunity to have a real impact on helping reform the criminal justice system. I asked for more time to consider the appointment. Apparently the President became irritated with my indecision and I later received a call from the White House that he was appointing Don Lay. In retrospect, I am amazed at how I could have passed up this opportunity. I have tried to analyze my own state of mind. Most lawyers would almost kill for an appointment to the second highest court in the land. Motivation is difficult to define. Many thoughts flew through my mind. First, I was in the midst of a campaign for the U. S. Senate, the outcome of which had not yet been decided and I did not understand why the President had moved the announcement ahead of the election. I did not like the ethics of holding the appointment open to the end of my term as Governor. I had the erroneous idea that after serving three successful terms as Governor, I could write my own ticket. I later discovered that after leaving the seat of power, most of your opportunities vanish. I also relished the idea of going into law practice with my son Biff in Omaha. Later I discovered, however, in jury trials, that my former success with juries had vanished. People regarded me as a politician and not a dedicated lawyer. There were always a few jurors who erroneously regarded you as suspect for having held elective office.

I had an interesting visit with President Johnson personally in Austin, Texas on January 2, 1967. I was flying back from New Orleans where I had attended the Sugar Bowl football game. We were flying over Austin, and I asked the pilot to set down as I would like to see Governor Connally of Texas. Upon arriving at the Governor's office, John informed me that "he" was in town. I knew what that pronoun meant. The President had a fully equipped condominium in the Federal Building. I was leaving the Governor's office in a few days and was planning to enter law practice with my son in Omaha. The President wanted to have lunch with Connally and me. The Governor discussed my accepting a federal appointment, including Attorney General. Johnson was waiting for us at his condo. When the Governor, the President, and I sat down for lunch. He asked the cook to come in and join us for the purpose of saying grace for us. It struck me odd that the most powerful man on earth found it necessary to call on someone else to communicate with his creator.

During this meeting, the President asked me if I would like a federal appointment after having passed up a judgeship on the 8th Circuit Court of Appeals. I replied yes, I would like to be appointed to the Supreme Court. He laughed, brushed it off, and said he was saving that one for Connally.

Prior to the Nebraska Primary in the spring of 1968, I was sitting with Maxine in our Omaha apartment one night when the phone rang. I was accustomed to the fact that when I received a call from the White House the first voice I heard was that of a staff member. This time it was President Johnson himself. He said, "Frank, Lady Bird and I are sitting here talking. We have read a poll which shows that if the primary were held today in Nebraska, that Bobby Kennedy would beat me. What do you think?"

I replied that the poll was probably accurate and that it would be necessary for him to do a great deal of work. I was not wise enough at that time to tell him it was hopeless. I still thought erroneously there was some way he could justify the Vietnam War. Sometime later I received a call from the White House telling me the President was going on television announcing that he would not be a candidate for reelection. I knew then that the thought of being defeated by Bobby Kennedy was more than he could take.

The power behind the Civil Rights Act, the Great Society, and a host of other social legislation had been brought down by a war which could have been prevented by using modern communication to exchange views with Ho Chi Ming and discover the ultimate truth.

The Johnson Space Center in Houston, however, stands as a lasting tribute to a leader who followed Kennedy in writing the next chapter in human travel into outer space.

Personalities

I would like to characterize some of the people and personalities that I encountered before I became Governor that in various ways became a part of my administration and after.

One was a young Irishman from my wife's hometown of Greeley, Nebraska, Frank Barrett. He was a graduate of the University of Nebraska College of Law. While he was still in law school, my partner, "Dugie" Doyle, hired him to work for the law firm investigating accidents that involved the Lincoln Traction Company. Then he was to write up the report. This was when I first became acquainted with him.

Barrett was a typical Irish man who couldn't have been more typical had he come directly from the old sod. His father was a lawyer and county judge in Greeley, Nebraska. His mother was a real character, an activist in the Democratic party, and for years postmaster in Greeley, Nebraska. She would bristle up anytime anybody referred to her as a postmistress. She would say "I am not anybody's mistress. I am the postmaster at Greeley, Nebraska."

Frank was a diligent worker and did a good job. When I became a candidate for Governor, Jim Exon mustered him into the organization. He was very active during the campaign including going out with a sound truck to give talks on behalf of the Morrison candidacy.

Frank Barrett had a tremendous sense of humor and a wonderful philosophy of life. After I became Governor, I wanted him for Chief of Staff but he declined and said he would like to be Director of Insurance, so that was his job during my administration. This friendship and admiration for Frank Barrett has continued all through my governorship and up to the present time.

In 1959, I met a young architectural student at the University of Nebraska by the name of Dick Youngscap. He was dating our daughter during her senior year at Lincoln High School. Dick was a handsome young man with dark fiery animated eyes that could pierce anyone. He had a burning ambition, many leadership qualities, and an inquiring penetrating mind. One evening when he came to the house for Jeannie, he complained bitterly about the way they operated the University of Nebraska. He said they were a bunch of blue-nosed hypocrites that have reflected the unimaginative character of the state and that they were more concerned about the minutia of human conduct than they were about anything creative and imaginative. I finally discovered that his immediate problem was that the University had placed his fraternity, the Phi Delts, on probation for having a beer party. He was complaining about the state of Nebraska not having any leadership and the University being maladministered. I said "Dick, don't you think that your fraternity has the unique opportunity to provide leadership if you think there is none?" I said, "What's your fraternity doing about that?" He hesitated a minute and said they were having a lot of fun. I said, "What are you doing about meeting this challenge? Why don't you go up to the University and tell them how they ought to run the place?" He replied that it wouldn't do any good. My response was, "How do you know if you don't try?" He didn't think that would have any effect. So I said, "As far as leadership in the state is concerned, haven't you got a great opportunity to provide that leadership?"

First thing I knew, Dick did go up to the University and start making friends, particularly my old friend Burt Smith, the head of the Department of Architecture, and Patrick Horsbrugh, an Englishman who is one of the most unique characters I have ever known and a tremendous advocate for preserving and enhancing the environment. Dick seemed to be taking on a new lease on life. At the next meeting of the fraternity where they elected officers for the incoming year, Dick nominated himself for president of the fraternity with an agenda for action. He was elected, and I saw a change in his attitude. Dick was the first person some time after this to come back and say to me, "Morrison, what are you doing about the leadership in the state?" I didn't totally agree with him that the state was without leadership, but he said, "Why don't you run for Governor?" When I did decide to run, after Jim Exon's coercion, Dick became an intimate member of the campaign team.

After I became Governor, he graduated from architecture school. He landscaped the Governor's mansion, became interested in landscaping on the interstate highway, became a leading architect in Lincoln, designed St. Elizabeth's Hospital, went on to develop the Firethorn Addition to Lincoln, and designed with Crenshaw the golf course in the Sandhills, a project nobody else had ever attempted.

Vonda Olson was a young secretary who came to work for Doyle, Morrison and Doyle right out of high school. She developed into a wonderful secretary. She was married to a young man by the name of Paul Olson. Vonda became an invaluable secretary in the law office and later in the governor's office.

One of the hard core members of the team Exon put together was Jack Obbink. Jack was over six feet tall, with a tremendous athletic body. He was a slow talking, deliberate young man who immediately commanded respect and had indomitable courage. He had been, I think, on the Battan Death March and for almost four years had been a Japanese prisoner of war during the Second World War. He had certain disabilities that hung over but you could never tell it by even the closest friendship and association with Jack. He had a long-standing friendship in the Optimist Club with Jim Exon.

Bill Davison was a cynical, delightful personality, who loved people and conversation. Bill was a gregarious sort and became an invaluable member of the advisory team in helping round up his friends in the Morrison campaign.

There was a local architect by the name of Fritz Verick who became campaign treasurer. Fritz's son-in-law was Clayton Yuetter, a world famous Republican. Fritz was highly professional, dignified, and one who inspired confidence from the beginning. One of the interesting incidents that happened during my primary campaign for the Democratic nomination concerned a woman by the name of Ila Story. She was active in the labor movement and was a strong supporter of Robert Conrad, my opponent. In the course of making telephone calls in support of Conrad, she started attacking Morrison's qualifications for the job. One of the people she got on the telephone was Fritz. Unmindful of his connection with the Morrison campaign, she started to give him a sales pitch for Bob Conrad when she said, "You know that Morrison would be a terrible Governor. Did you ever know how sloppy he dresses? In everything he does, he's a real slob when it comes to the way he puts himself together and his clothing and so forth. He'd be just that way as Governor." After painting this less than complimentary picture of Morrison, Fritz notified her on the phone that he was Morrison's campaign treasurer and active in the Morrison campaign, which seemed to end that conversation.

It was rather interesting that Fritz's son-in-law, Clayton Yuetter, later was to become one of the most prominent Republican leaders in the United States. Clayton was born and grew up in Frontier County where I served as county attorney. He started out as a member of Norbert Tiemann's staff when he was Governor and skyrocketed up the ladder. He was Assistant Secretary of

Agriculture, became trade representative for the United States, and then Chairman of the Republican National Committee.

There was Frank Sands from the Gering-Scottsbluff area, and Clive Short from Chadron who were friends from the Panhandle. Both of them were small, wiry, cocky, sharp, aggressive people who were invaluable during the campaign. Short was a contractor and had done quite a bit of building in eastern Wyoming, the northwestern part of Nebraska, and probably some up in South Dakota. Short was instrumental in getting Sands to switch from Conrad to Morrison during the campaign.

There were many other people. One of the people who was active in the campaign was Josephine Fisher, wife of Lincoln's City Engineer Carl Fisher. Josephine was a northwest Nebraska girl who grew up at Harrison. She was one of the hardest working, most diligent and knowledgeable people I have ever known. She had worked for the Legislature near the legislative process and had a photographic mind. Her avocation was raising bulldogs. She raised some of the finest bulldogs you would find anywhere in the United States. Those bulldogs appealed to Josephine. I think they had the same set of jaw, only Josephine was much more handsome than a bulldog. The characteristic of determination and dedication made her invaluable, not only during the campaign but when I became Governor. She was a very important member of my inner staff. She became acquainted with all bills introduced in the Legislature. She knew the legislative process from A to Z. After I became Governor, I relied upon Jo a great deal to analyze the contents of bills, track their progress through the Legislature, and discuss them with me. There is no way that I can fully express the invaluable role that Josephine played in coordination between the legislative process and the Governor's office.

One of the original invaluable members of the Morrison team was Jerry Hassett. At the time, Jerry was unmarried and devoted to his sister Mary. The two of them were inseparable. Jerry was a devout Roman Catholic. His acquaintanship in the City of Omaha was extensive. He knew the background and temperament and a part of the resume of most of the leaders in both political parties in Omaha. Jerry was a person who formed friendships that lasted for a lifetime. In making arrangements, setting up appearances, and all during the campaign, his leadership in Omaha was invaluable. I don't know how we would possibly have functioned as we did in the City of Omaha without the leadership and hard work of Jerry Hassett. Later I appointed him Election Commissioner in Douglas County.

After my election as Governor, one of the people I called on for counsel, legal advice, and to assist with speech writing, was an old friend of mine from law school days who had one of the best legal minds I have ever encountered. Bert Overcash was a partner in the Woods Law Firm in Lincoln. He was a dedicated, loyal friend who was endowed with tremendous amounts of common sense and intellectual honesty. He would tell you exactly what he thought. He was invaluable in helping me draft my first address to the Legislature and served as my legal counsel all during my term as Governor. There is no way that I could thank Bert adequately for his service. Never once did he make any demands for himself. He served both the State of Nebraska and myself without pay or compensation. All of these facts were generally unknown to the public, and he is one of the unsung heroes of the Morrison administration.

One of the invaluable members of the Morrison administration was a young former teacher and house builder from Kearney, Nebraska who understood the state Legislature, understood the legislative process, and in addition to that, chaired the Educational Committee of the state legislature. Norm Otto was of German descent, had the tall, lean, hungry look of impeccable honesty and integrity, and possessed a burning desire for public service. He had been a candidate for Lieutenant Governor and was defeated. He was a supporter of my opponent in the Democratic primary for Governor. I was only slightly acquainted with him, but I knew of his service in the Legislature, his chairmanship of the Educational Committee, his fierce loyalty to people and friends, and his basic honesty. With this kind of a background, he had those ingredients that I wanted for my Administrative Assistant.[33] I gave Norm the job and never regretted it. He served during the first two years of my administration but decided he wanted to become Small Business Administrator for the State of Nebraska, so he resigned to take that job.

Two people whom I recruited for public service were men I had known before I became Governor. Neither of them was active in my campaign. Both were registered Republicans. One was a retired banker, Byron Dunn. I first encountered him when he was president of the National Bank of Commerce in Lincoln. He showed up representing the bank in the probate proceedings of my original benefactor in the Maywood area. That was when I recognized that Byron Dunn was a workhorse. He had a high degree of intelligence and was dedicated to serve his employer's interest. He was retired when I became Governor. He had been active as a volunteer in promoting educational television in Nebraska and was interested in promoting Nebraska, particularly in educational television and economic development advancement of tourism. He rendered invaluable service, all without any cost to the state.

The other man was Nathan Gold, a Lincoln merchant. At the time I was elected Governor, my wife was fashion coordinator for Gold's Department Store and a buyer for Gold's store in certain areas of merchandise. Nathan Gold was a giant of a man who was dedicated to the promotion of the economic interests of Nebraska and to the development of the youth in the state. He was active in providing annual banquets for 4-H Club winners and bidding on prize animals shown at the State Fair by 4-H clubbers. He was an anonymous benefactor in various charities and he was a tremendously talented business executive. Nathan Gold headed up what was known as Nebraska's Resources Commission.

David Osterhoudt was the paid executive director of an independent organization to promote state economic development. This organization's board of directors was appointed by the governor. I used this organization as an effective tool to work toward such development.

I inherited from the Brooks administration one of the most remarkable people I have ever known, a professional secretary by the name of Sally Gordon. She was much more than a perfect typist or woman capable of taking dictation without error. She knew and understood people, was full of common sense, and, at times, invaluable in giving advice. I think Sally at the time was barely past fifty years of age and was an invaluable member of the secretarial pool in our team for the operation of state government. Today, at 94, Sally is still working as an assistant at arms in the legislature. Her vitality is amazing.

After months of deliberation, I decided to keep as State Highway Engineer a man by the name of Hossick. I had my own ideas about a highway program and since Hossick had been appointed and indoctrinated by a previous administration, I had considered appointing a new man.

Pearl Finnegan, who was a member of the Brooks administration as Director of Agriculture, was a dynamic young man who had spent a lot of time with the Southwest Research Institute of Kansas City in promoting new uses for agricultural products. Ethanol was then far in the distance and not an accepted additive for gasoline. He worked closely with Roy Welch, an Omaha grain man and partner of U.S. Senator Hugh Butler, who early promoted the idea of using ethanol.

Republican George Morris, who had been one of the orphans shipped into Nebraska at one time, had become active in my campaign for Governor and headed up the organization Republicans for Morrison. He was a man of considerable ability and confidence in his own ability to administer and formulate policy.

George Morris was ap unique personality. I had endorsed successfully an abolition of the existing form of administration of state institutions by a control board of three people appointed by the governor. I thought this sometimes injected too much political maneuvering into the administration of state institutions. I felt administration should be put on a more professional basis. The board was abolished and the Legislature set up a new method of administering state institutions in the form of a director of state institutions, together with an advisory board to the governor. I appointed George Morris to this position and I think it proved, even though he was controversial, to be a wise appointment. We almost instantly set into motion expanded educational programs for inmates.

Gene Budig, a graduate of the University of Nebraska, was a 24-year-old reporter for the *Lincoln Star*. He had grown up with our kids in McCook. I first met him when he was fourteen and looking for an Adlai Stephenson campaign button. He covered the Statehouse for the *Star* when I was Governor. When Otto left as Chief of Staff, I appointed Budig as the youngest Chief of Staff in the nation. He went on to become president of three major universities, a member of the President's Council on Higher Education, President of the American League, advisor to Major League Baseball, and a member of the Princeton University faculty.

With appointment of other members of the team, the Morrison administration was ready to roll. I brought into the administration a number of young men. I put a man by the name of Ron Jensen in charge of a new agency called the Commission on Aging.

David Evans, a college student, was under the Eagleton program from Rutgers University in New Jersey and was not paid by the state of Nebraska. His mission was to learn about state government and he was used on all aspects of the office.

President Johnson had launched a vast program known as the War on Poverty. Our legislature had created a new state agency to implement this program. This agency was placed under the governor's office. Paul Moss and Hess Dyas worked on implementing a variety of programs to improve the lot of the poor. Our program for bringing new industries into the state did more to help in this area than our program called War on Poverty. I spent little time on this aspect of my administration because I felt it did little good.

Two young women, Jeanie Fellows and Sharon Crouse, worked closely with us from such agencies as the Park, Fish and Game Commission.

I selected John Mitchell as chairman of the State Democratic Party. He became a leading lawyer, radio executive and a valuable board member of the Great Platte River Road Archway Memorial Foundation.

The new administration was predominantly youthful; however, there was a combination of youth and maturity in the important posts of state government. I frequently told people that I don't care whether you are eight or eighty. If you have some creative ideas that will help us on the road to progress, I want to hear from you. I don't care whether you call yourself a Republican or a Democrat, a progressive, a conservative, or a liberal. The important thing is that you have ideas that will be useful in promoting progress and helping us solve our problems.

Consequently, many people who gravitated to the administration who were very helpful. One was Eleanor Enerson. She had a deep emotional commitment to the whole mentally retarded program. I told her one day that as important as this was, it might be even more important to appoint a committee to deal with the problems of the gifted child because these children had so much to offer and sometimes they were neglected and not inspired to develop their full potential. She said, "I agree, and I have a person who ought to head up a committee. She is the wife of my husband's partner and her name is Clark." So I contacted Mrs. Clark immediately and put her in charge of a new committee to promote programs to develop the potential of gifted children.

Five months into my first administration, we had a wonderful experience. It was June and we were getting ready to celebrate our 25th wedding anniversary when we received news that our first grandchild was born: John Martin Morrison. What a thrill that was.

It was during this month that we also attended our first Governors' Conference which was held in Honolulu. We flew over in the Minnesota National Guard plane where we were accompanied by Governor Nutter, the newly elected Governor of Montana and his staff. This was my first opportunity to meet and discuss policy with all of the other governors who had assembled in Honolulu for the National Governors Conference. There were many others to follow.

---

33 This position in the Governor's office is now called Chief of Staff.

Family

Many people on my trip have not only inspired me but have helped others along the road. I owe a great debt of gratitude to them and to the wonderful family and relatives it was my good fortune to have.

I could never repay the debt I owe my mother and her parents. The debt I owe my mother's sister, Edna Brenner Snyder, is monumental. She made my legal education at the University of Nebraska possible. As a mother and teacher, she was a role model for all of us.

Bill, one of her boys, was killed in World War II. Her oldest son was like a young brother. He became an outstanding lawyer in Colorado and inspired his son to follow him.

Charlotte, the only daughter, married Hank DeArmond, a Los Angeles banker, mothered a wonderful daughter, and became a leading professional woman in California.

My Uncle Tice was father to one of the most remarkable women I have ever known. Margaret, the mother of three girls, was married to a rancher, Henry Garat. Margaret's self-sacrifice, discipline, and hard work to develop her full potential to serve her family and others created a new benchmark as a role model.

Words are totally inadequate to relate what my own family has meant to me. The nineteen-year-old beauty I met in Stockville, Nebraska on the Fourth of July, 1935 was to change my life forever. This country school teacher had a voice which, if properly trained, would have dominated the Metropolitan. In my political life, she has been my greatest supporter. Her supporting role as wife of a public figure attracted national attention, and she was named chair of the Governors' Wives of the United States. Her singing attracted national attention. She was a soloist at both the New York and Seattle World's Fairs during my terms as Governor. She became a leader in Arbor Day celebrations and a radio and television personality. Above all of that, she has been a superb homemaker, mother, and creator of a refuge for her husband and three children.

The lives of the three children Maxine mothered vastly improved the quality of my trip. Frank Jr. (Biff), became a leader in his profession and added a great deal to the quality of case law in America. His compassion for others and his dedication to giving back to his hometown of McCook, his own leadership and material gifts, fills my heart with gratitude. He and Sharon have given us two wonderful grandchildren. Ann Elizabeth is a Broadway actress, and John Martin is a leading trial lawyer in Montana who aspires to public service.

Our son, David Jon, has a creative mind. He saw the waste of fuel through air resistance and invented a nose cone for trucks. He saw the waste of material in hotel soap bars and created a press to enlarge the bar without increasing the material. He has considerable talent as a painter. He is the father of two quality children, Jeanne Eschefelder, a Houston nurse, and Clayton Frank Morrison, a Houston businessman.

Our daughter, Jean Marie Galloway, from the day she was born, was a human magnet, high school homecoming queen, and a member of Dr. Don Clifton's project of selecting high school students with outstanding people skills as educational tools. She is married to Dr. Ben Galloway, a noted forensic pathologist in Denver. She is mother of Cynthia Ann, a Denver business woman and Katherine Jean, of Paris, France, an advertising specialist. Jean is immediate past chair of the Volunteers of America, a television executive who is dedicating her life to charitable causes.

My sister, Hope, became an integral part of our family. Her hard work and dedication to her family were remarkable. After her divorce and moving to McCook, she became a licensed practical nurse and an important part of the healthy delivery services at St.Catherine's Hospital in McCook. My mother's last years were made more meaningful as housekeeper and caregiver to Hope's children up until the time of Viva's death. Hope's children became wonderful role models - Sarah as an accomplished secretary, mother and grandmother; and Bill who, after graduation from the University of Nebraska, attended St. Paul's seminary in Kansas City, from which he later received his Doctor's degree after two years as a missionary in Africa. He is now the Methodist minister in Minden, Nebraska. He and his wife, Cathy, have three grown children of their own and one adopted handicapped child named Hope. My sister Hope died at age 92 on her mother's wedding anniversary.

Heritage Square

Among my concerns as we entered the last decade of the twentieth century was youth picking the wrong role models, if any, and lacking a knowledge of history.

The great philosopher George Santayana once said, "Those who cannot remember the past are condemned to repeat it."[34] Because of his use of the word condemned, I assume he referred to the mistakes of the past. As a child I was taught the precept,

> "Lives of great men all remind us
> We can make our lives sublime.
> And, departing, leave behind us
> Footprints on the sands of time."[35]

In today's world, far too often dominated by cynicism, violence, sensualism and materialism, my ambition was to call our attention to our heritage of self-sacrifice, compassion, service, and responsibility for the common good as an ideal.

When our son Biff moved to Whitefish, Montana in 1969, he took part in a movement to revitalize the town. In 1997 he started a movement to help revitalize his native town of McCook. He enlisted my efforts to create what my wife Maxine named Heritage Square.

The George W. Norris Home in McCook was preserved as a State Park. Located between G and H Streets on the west side of Norris Avenue, it faces the city park which bares his name.

Probably no U.S. Senator in the history of the nation ever had a greater positive impact on American life than Senator George W. Norris of McCook, Nebraska. The Norris-Rayburn Act which electrified rural America helped end de facto slavery of farm women. The Tennessee Valley Authority helped convert a poverty stricken region of America into prosperity. The Norris-LaGuardia Act elevated the position of labor. The Lame Duck Amendment to the Constitution improved legislative responsibility. Norris' fathership on Nebraska's non-partisan one house legislature and his dedication to protecting our natural resources for the benefit of all of the people against exploitation by a few marked him as a role model for the nation. In 1927 George Norris made a statement which I felt should be the compass for every public servant in America: "The only pay for service that is worthwhile is a satisfied conscience. I would rather be right in my own heart than to have the approval of the whole world."

Biff bought the property on the north side of the Park including the Hoyt House at 105 H Street. Amongst Biff, our son David Jon and myself, we have remodeled it into a Morrison Home.

In cooperation with Van Correll, a McCook banker, we acquired title to the old abandoned greenhouse facing Norris Avenue and offered it to Governor Ben Nelson as a site on which to move his boyhood home.

Ralph Brooks was a graduate lawyer who spent his entire life in education. While he was Superintendent of the McCook School System and President of McCook College, Ralph Brooks was elected Governor of Nebraska. All three Nebraska governors from McCook were disciples of Senator Norris.

Biff and his mother Maxine incorporated the Frank B. Morrison Family Educational Foundation to help promote Heritage Square and positive educational programs in the area.

In cooperation with the McCook School System, we are promoting a walk from the High Plains Museum, past the historic Courthouse, then continuing past the only house in Nebraska designed by the famous architect, Frank Lloyd Wright, on to the Nelson home, the Norris home, the city library, and ending at the Morrison Home. A proper memorial to the late Ralph Brooks is in the works. This area has been designated as Heritage Square. The primary object is to interest people in public service and their positive heritage.

In addition to Heritage Square, the Frank B. Morrison Family Educational Foundation is starting a program to have all high school seniors in McCook write essays each year and vote on the teacher who had the greatest positive impact on their life during their twelve years of school. This winning teacher would be honored by a community banquet, a cash honorarium and a recognition plaque. All of this to emphasize the importance of the teacher in our culture. If successful, it could spread to other schools.

This and the Great Platte River Road Memorial Archway project became my retirement recreation.

34 The Life of Reason, vol. I, Reason in Common Sense, 1905-1906.

35 Henry Wadsworth Longfellow, A Psalm of Life, 1839.

Conclusion

I have now completed my conscious trip through the 20th century. My personal experiences have been augmented by information I have received from others and from recorded history. For the evaluation of those who follow me, I would like to register some of my conclusions from this trip which I seldom, if ever, hear policymakers discuss.

1. Human beings are the only creatures with power to use the forces of nature for our own ennoblement or the destruction of our species.

2. Admiral Rickover's testimony before Congress that he thought the race would commit suicide through nuclear war brought back personal experiences. I have sat in the commanding general's office of the Strategic Air Command with the President of the United States, knowing he was vested with the power to destroy all human life on this planet by nuclear detonation. This convinced me that these weapons must be abolished from the face of the earth. No human being or combination of humans should have this power.

3. Next to preventing fatal contamination of the atmosphere with radioactive fallout, is polluting it with sufficient gases to bring on global warming or other conditions endangering life on this planet.

4. The population explosion must be checked without sacrificing the sacred aspect of human life through abortion, ethnic cleansing, mass homicide, and war.

5. We must build a more just, effective, and meaningful criminal justice system.

6. We must explore the secrets of human motivation and the emotions of revenge, hate, envy, greed, and paranoia, all of which hamper human cooperation and progress.

7. We must create an economic, cultural, and educational system which will inspire, motivate, and make possible the full intellectual development of every child. The human mind, we now know, has the potential to harness the forces of nature to usher in a vast new era of quality life on this planet heretofore undreamed of.

8. We must prevent confusion in the information age by creating mechanisms for discovery of the truth.

9. We must perfect our economic system to provide equal opportunity, not equal wealth, for every person.

10. We must create additional dispute resolution mechanisms to reduce violence to an absolute minimum.

11. We must utilize our educational plants twelve months out of the year to mobilize our youth in a vast crusade of competence so they can deal with the vexing problems and opportunities of the new century - cultural, economic, and spiritual.

12. We must convince the people of the world of our common humanity, and that we are all shipmates on this ship we call earth, flying through the cosmos with one common destiny.

13. We must invent new mechanisms for dispute resolutions between individuals and nations. General McArthur's statement that modern technology has made war obsolete must be taken to heart. The wholesale killing, crippling, and blinding of innocent civilians and children as a way to punish errant heads of state is a form of barbarism civilization should no longer tolerate.

14. A revered American president once said this nation cannot long exist half free and half slave. Our revered capitalistic democracy will eventually collapse in a world where the vast majority of its people live in poverty, functional illiteracy and filth. Masses of people are ill-nourished, ill-clad, ill-housed and suffering from preventable disease. The vast majority of the world's people do not have access to those things which the minority consider essentials. Modern science, technology, enlightened banking and political policies can reverse, if not entirely cure, this condition. It cannot be done by political, business and religious leaders who pander to our parochial and selfish instincts. A challenge to American education in the

21st century is to discover, motivate, inspire and develop leadership which can teach the world how to elevate the quality of life for all people.

My conscious existence on this planet is coming to an end. The new millennium may well determine whether the human species is worthy of survival. I am convinced it is. Hundreds of various attempts have been made throughout history for individuals to escape the problems of this earth to a place called Heaven. Many different religions have grown up to define the purpose of life, guarantee its immortality, and describe our creator some call God, others Allah, others Deo, and others the Great Spirit. To obey his commands, they have drafted rules of conduct seldom adhered to.

I have come to the conclusion that the greatest challenge to our political institutions in the new millennium is to formulate and execute policies which will elevate our collective conduct to the point where we are worthy of immortality.

Index

Republican River 59
Republicans (Party) 5, 11, 16, 21, 23, 26, 40, 48, 51, 53, 56, 58, 68, 70, 84,
                     88, 89, 94, 95, 98, 126, 132, 147, 159, 166, 173, 175,
                     176, 178
Rock Island Railroad 6, 11, 22, 23
Roosevelt, Franklin D. 51, 54, 56, 58, 68-70, 75, 84, 87, 118
Roosevelt, Theodore 11, 15, 40

Sands, Frank 174
Seaton, Fred 17, 38, 47, 159
Scottsbluff, NE 3, 94, 174
Snyder, Flora Edna Brenner 33
Snyder, M.J. 33
Snyder, Paul 24, 33
Sorenson, C. A. 95
Sorenson, Phil 113
Sorenson, Ted 95, 96
South Platte River 3, 6
Stephenson, Adlai 89, 157, 177
Stockville, NE 53, 54, 56, 57, 58, 59, 60, 62, 63-73, 83, 179

Taft, William H. 15, 50
Truman, Harry 84, 87, 88, 89, 91, 105

University of Nebraska 4, 34, 37, 38, 40, 41, 42, 46, 47, 48, 50, 58, 62, 66,
                       79, 87, 93, 95, 99, 100, 104, 107, 138, 152, 153, 154,
                       171, 172, 177, 179, 180

Van Pelt, Robert 57, 71, 73
Vietnam 112, 113, 114, 130, 132, 133, 136, 137, 138, 139, 142, 167, 169

Weaver, Phil 90
Wheeler, Burton 69, 70
Wildcat Creek 6, 11-15, 36, 42, 168
Wilson, Woodrow 11, 15, 23, 25, 42

Youngman, Lawrence 32, 40, 62, 120
Youngscap, Dick 172
Yuetter, Clayton 173